THE E³ EFFECT

The E³ Effect
A Proven Blueprint for Building World-Class Teams

Daniel Roth

©2025 All Rights Reserved. No portion of this book may be reproduced, stored in a retrieval system, or transmitted in any form or by any means—electronic, mechanical, photocopy, recording, scanning, or other—except for brief quotations in critical reviews or articles without the prior permission of the author.

Published by Game Changer Publishing

Paperback ISBN: 978-1-968250-39-3
Hardcover ISBN: 978-1-968250-40-9
Digital ISBN: 978-1-968250-41-6

www.GameChangerPublishing.com

What Leaders Are Saying

"During Daniel Roth's decade on my executive team, I witnessed his exceptional ability to transform complex customer experience challenges into clear, actionable strategies. His inspirational leadership style empowers teams to reimagine what's possible in customer service. Daniel's strategic brilliance in the CX space, combined with his talent for distilling intricate problems into elegant solutions, makes him one of the most effective business leaders I've worked alongside."

—Rick Ferry, Former CEO, Aegis and C3

"As a CEO in the CX analytics space, I've had the privilege of working with Daniel Roth across multiple organizations since 2020. What sets Daniel apart is his rare ability to bridge the strategic and tactical. He brings visionary thinking that elevates employee, customer, and partner experiences while ensuring every initiative translates into measurable ROI. I witnessed this firsthand during his breakthrough work at DispatchHealth, where his multi-modal approach reduced trivial calls, improved CX scores, and cut operational costs. He used data to inform high-level decisions, demonstrating how analytics can drive strategic direction. His leadership style is authentic and effective, whether addressing the C-suite or frontline teams. Daniel operates with integrity and empathy and delivers results that last."

—Dan Dougherty, Partner, CatalyzeCX

"I've had the pleasure of working side by side with Daniel and, more recently, partnering with him on CX solutions for clients. His dynamic leadership, problem-solving mindset, and ability to future-proof organizations set him apart. Daniel distills world-class team leadership into clear, actionable phases centered around psychological safety, purposeful vulnerability, and shared purpose. His framework transforms teams from baseline performance to high-functioning innovation. This is a real-world model that fosters trust, collaboration, and cultural alignment."

—Tom Moroney, Co-Founder and Managing Partner,
North America, Access CX

"Getting inside the mind of Daniel Roth is a rare and amazing opportunity. This book reveals how he thinks, how he leads, and how he drives innovation. Apply his methods in your own world and watch how empathetic and visionary execution can transform your business."

—Andrew Pryfogle, Head of CX/AI and Global Education Lead, AVANT Communications

"Having worked alongside Daniel Roth for three years, I experienced firsthand the power of the E³ Effect. This is not just a framework; it is a living, breathing approach to leadership grounded in clarity, purpose, and direction. It creates deep accountability, empathy, and connection, and it celebrates growth through both challenges and wins. The E³ Effect changed how I lead and how I think about collaboration and team performance."

—Michael Hildebrand, Director, Workforce Services, SynapseHealth

"I had the pleasure of working with Daniel for fifteen years. In this book, he articulates the E³ Effect with clarity and depth. Having collaborated closely with him, I've seen its transformative power firsthand. Its beauty lies in its simplicity and its ability to help executives build high-performing, successful teams by enabling, empowering, and encouraging meaningful endeavor."

—Ken Epstein, Partner, P3

"Daniel's leadership has significantly elevated my own approach. His ability to enable, empower, and execute has strengthened our partnership and inspired me to pursue greater strategic impact. He consistently builds exceptional teams that deliver."

—Jason Rodriguez, Vice President, Integrated Solutions, TTEC

"I've seen firsthand how Daniel's formula for success works. We used these same principles to completely transform our Customer Care Access Center team at DispatchHealth and made it world-class. Absolutely stellar. Simple but powerful."

—Michael King, Director of Operations, SynapseHealth

"Having worked side by side with Daniel Roth, I can attest to the mastery presented in this book. He leads with clarity, adapts to change, and crafts content that resonates with visual, auditory, and kinesthetic learners alike."

—Erin Denholm, President, Denholm & Associates Consulting LLC

"From the moment I met Daniel over a decade ago, I was struck by his ability to articulate a clear and compelling vision. He doesn't just see the big picture; he outlines the step-by-step path to get there with calm confidence. His leadership inspires trust and clarity, and with him, success doesn't just feel possible, it feels inevitable."

—Sue Silva, Owner, Superus Marketing

"Daniel has been a driving force behind every milestone we've reached together. His perseverance, strategic insight, and commitment to excellence have elevated our achievements and deepened the trust that fuels our partnership."

—Mille Lozano, Vice President of Operations, BPO

"Daniel Roth is an exceptional leader whose integrity, fairness, and strategic insight bring out the best in teams. He inspires peak performance and delivers consistent, values-driven results. The E^3 *Effect is a game-changer for any organization."*

—Arnie Roza, Partner, Innovative Solutions Consulting and Predictive Index

"I had the privilege of working with Daniel for many years and consistently witnessed his exceptional leadership. His smart, scalable solutions improved engagement, performance, and revenue. Daniel is a powerful coach whose integrity inspires."

—Michelle Roza, CPC, Love Breakthrough Coach, Heart's Desire International

"Daniel has a special ability to take seemingly impossible tasks and turn them into reality by empowering people to exceed their own expectations. Whether in healthcare or food service, with large or small teams, Daniel starts with what matters: the individuals doing the work and the leaders guiding them. His ability to break down complex projects into clear, actionable steps has a lasting impact that extends far beyond his direct involvement."

—Bill McCarthy, Director of Operational Planning & Analysis,
Tractor Supply Company

"Leveraging decades of cross-industry experience, Daniel Roth has created a leadership framework that fosters deep engagement and emotional connection within teams, anchored by technology and designed to drive high performance."

—Justin Scambray, CEO, WellHaven Pet Health

A PROVEN BLUEPRINT FOR
BUILDING WORLD CLASS TEAMS

THE E^3 EFFECT

ENABLE, EMPOWER
& ~~EXECUTE~~ *ENDEAVOR*

DANIEL ROTH

For Aston

Aston, your drive to serve something greater than yourself—and the heart you bring to that mission—moves me beyond words.

As you pursue your path in International Relations, keep asking the questions others miss. Keep uncovering the challenges that matter. And keep showing us what's possible when knowledge, empathy, and intention come together in service of a better world.

Be the difference. Carry the standard. Lead with integrity, always.

I stand proudly beside you, as your father, your biggest believer, and your fiercest fan.

Love always,
Dad

Acknowledgments

This book is the result of many people pouring into my life, personally and professionally.

To the leaders and mentors who saw something in me before I saw it in myself, your belief planted the seeds of this journey and gave me the courage to forge my own path. Thank you for lighting the way, offering wisdom, and helping me step into my voice.

To Dawn and Aston, my foundation and my greatest source of strength: Your belief gives me the courage to dream big, your challenge helps me grow, and your presence turns vision into something real. Together, we're building a life that reflects who we are and the adventure we're here to live. You are the living embodiment of ***The E3 Effect***—enabling me with your trust, empowering me with your knowledge and love, and endeavoring beside me every step of the way.

To my publisher, thank you for your guidance, encouragement, and belief in this work. Without your support, this book would still be an idea waiting to be written. Your partnership gave this journey structure, momentum, and a voice beyond my own.

To Miguel Ramos, my mentor, teacher, former employer, and dear friend for over twenty-five years: Your generosity with ideas, humility in asking for mine, and enduring belief in who I am and who I can become have created space for me to flourish. You've helped shape the way I lead, listen, and grow. I'm better because of you, and this book carries your fingerprints throughout.

To every reader, thank you for choosing to lead with intention. May ***The E3 Effect*** inspire you to enable greatness in others, empower your voice, and endeavor with purpose in everything you do.

Foreword

It is uncommon to encounter someone who profoundly influences your perspective on leadership and leaves a lasting impact on your approach to business (and life). Daniel is one such individual for me, and I believe (I hope) I have also played a similar role in his journey. Since our collaboration commenced over two decades ago at Precision Response Corporation (PRC), Daniel has been more than just a colleague; he has been, as he often states, "a brother from another mother."

From the outset, Daniel exhibited a unique ability to see things differently. He consistently questioned, "How can we improve this?" and "Why is it done this way?" This mindset—curious, driven, and perpetually seeking progress—has propelled him from being a proficient problem-solver to becoming a visionary leader in the C-suite. Presently, as the founder of PangeaEffect, he offers his clients an exceptional blend of strategic vision, big-picture thinking, and practical execution.

I have had the honor of working with Daniel as he navigated new challenges and advanced into increasingly complex senior leadership roles. After leaving PRC, we somehow managed to continue collaborating, either within the same organization or as a client and partner to each other. What has rendered this journey memorable is the significant contributions he has made along the way. He constantly challenges me to think innovatively, raising the standards while leading with integrity and purpose. This is what differentiates Daniel: he does not merely step up; he reshapes the path forward.

Much like Pangea once unified the world's continents into a singular powerhouse, Daniel excels at integrating diverse talent, technology, and customer-centric strategies. Through his visionary leadership, he seamlessly connects global operations, ensuring exceptional customer experiences that transcend borders, akin to Pangea's influence.

In The E^3 Effect, Daniel shares the blueprint he has developed through years of valuable leadership and experience. This is not a collection of buzzwords, but a practical, insightful guide grounded in real-life lessons and meaningful achievements. Whether you are embarking on your leadership journey or seeking to elevate your team, you will discover impactful insights within these pages.

If you aspire to lead with intention and create something genuinely significant, let this book be the starting point of your journey.

Thank you, my esteemed colleague, friend, and brother!

– Miguel A. Ramos
Managing Partner
P3/Precision Point Partners, Inc.

Table of Contents

The E3 Effect Thematic Map

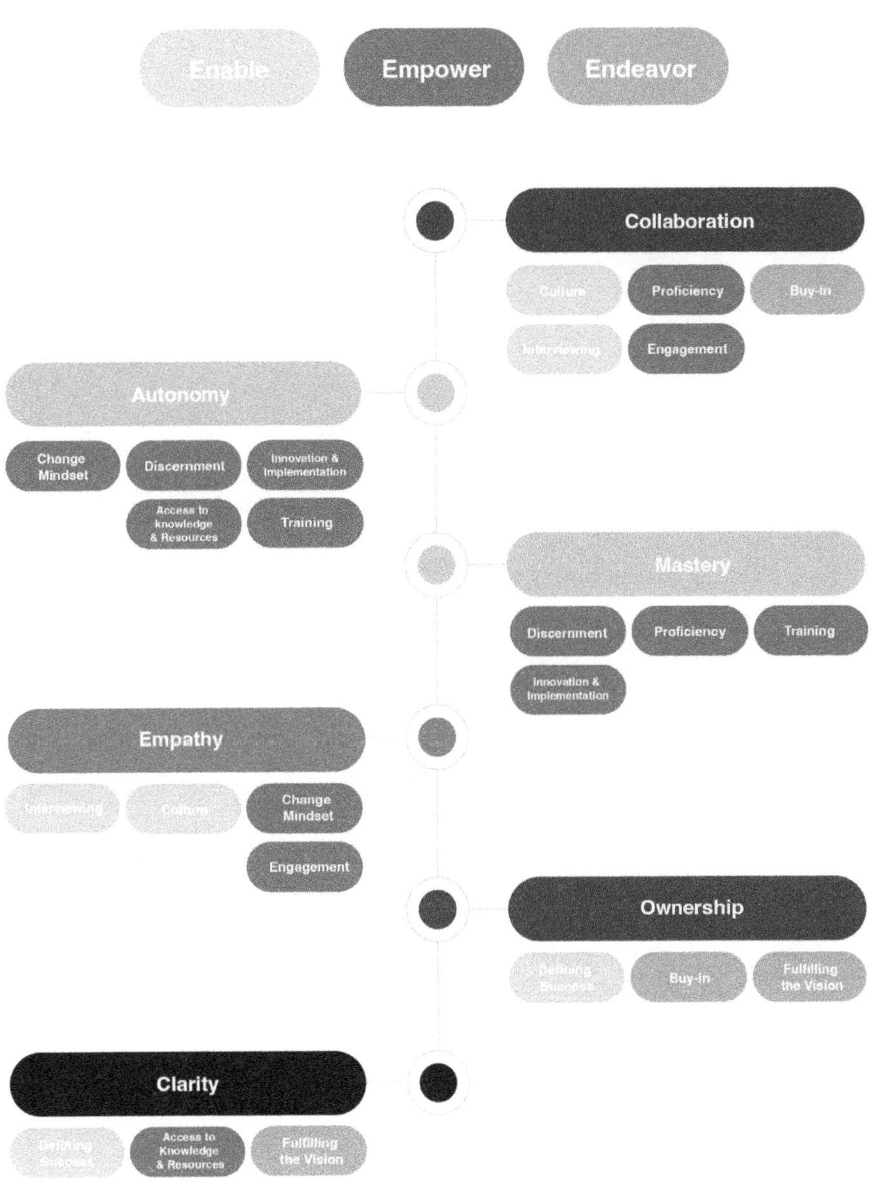

INTRODUCTION

You've likely picked up this book because you're searching—not for another trendy framework or recycled leadership theory, but for something that actually works. You've led teams, driven change, and experimented with strategies that promised transformation. Yet here you are—still wondering why culture feels so hard to sustain, why performance wavers, and why some teams never quite click the way they should.

If that sounds familiar, you're in the right place.

This book was written for leaders like you—seasoned, driven, and ready to cut through the noise. It's for the team builder who believes in potential but is tired of watching it stall. It's for the leader who values authenticity and is searching for tools that resonate with real people in real workplaces.

What you'll find here is not theory for theory's sake. You'll discover a proven, experience-tested blueprint: Enable, Empower, Endeavor (E3)—a performance rubric built for scale, sustainability, and the very human complexity of teams.

Throughout this book, we'll revisit the reader's core question: What actually works when it comes to leading high-performing teams and shaping a thriving culture? The chapters that follow will provide clarity, tools, and examples that honour your experience and guide your next steps.

Who Am I—and Why This Book?

At this point, you may be wondering: Who is this person telling me how to lead? Why should I listen?

I'm a CEO, Founder & Strategist, employee, husband, and father—a transformative thinker and strategist with over twenty-five years of experience leading teams of all sizes, from startups to global operations of ten thousand people. I've worked across fifteen industries—healthcare to logistics, fast food to retail—supporting top Fortune 500s and day-one startups.

My journey hasn't been linear. I grew up in a middle-class family, watched my parents divorce at age twelve, and spent my adolescence figuring out who I was and what I stood for. I've repeatedly chosen learning over comfort, attending seminars by Tony Robbins, studying under world-class leaders like Barack Obama, Oprah Winfrey, Richard Branson, and Colin Powell, and earning my Lean Six Sigma Black Belt to turn insight into measurable outcomes.

Every lesson I've learned about resilience, vision, systems, and people is embedded in this book.

In the 1990s, I was fortunate to join a financial company where my leader introduced me to self-improvement, taking me to a Tony Robbins seminar, "The Competitive Edge," which focused on business and personal performance strategies.

What I saw in Tony resonated with me. I saw elements of my own style in a way that ignited me. Watching his impact at an unimaginable level caused my brain to detach from all I knew to be possible about myself and look anew into an unknown future.

This relatable person brought boundless energy, free-flowing knowledge, sharing, and the ability to impart wisdom in a way that I could absorb, process, and effectuate. I've always been—and continue to be—a person of passion, a person of authenticity, and a person of results. Seeing the energy Tony was generating set me on a path to foster more of it in the world.

My journey began. Taking a path of continuous learning, attending personal and professional development with many extraordinary leaders, including Barack Obama, Oprah Winfrey, Richard Branson, Colin Powell, Adam Silver, Ashton Kutcher, Zig Ziglar, Wayne Dyer, and Horst Schulze, to name a few. In the early days, as I absorbed more, I committed to investing in myself as a way of life.

In my senior year, I moved out and worked full time, lived with my barely older brother, and still managed to get myself to school every single day and graduate. College was not a given. It was clear to me that being someone who made a difference for others and in the world was going to be my calling.

With parental encouragement, I went to college. I ended up dropping out later; I chose work over college. That's a story for a future book.

When I returned to college, I was on the leading edge of the online University of Phoenix phenomenon—an early adopter. That is who I am: a boundary pusher, a beta tester, someone who challenges limits, one comfortable in the unknown, a person who creates systems—and makes them doable, possible, effective, tangible, and workable in the real world.

Who Will Find This Book Useful?

It's for those who want to be part of something bigger than themselves. It's for the person who doesn't want to be mired in the everyday minutiae, and not just see the bigger picture, but live it.

This book is for the person who wants to see change and is willing to be the cause of that change. It is for someone who may not know how to create an opportunity but is willing to learn.

Why Should You Listen to Me?

I have gathered a broad set of experiences with more than twenty-five years in leadership, supporting fifteen industries—including healthcare, logistics, quick-serve restaurants, and retail—with companies ranging from top-five Fortune 500 firms to day-one startups. Some you may recognize: United Healthcare, FedEx, and Yum! Brands. Each role and each ecosystem has given me another tool in my toolbox. Observing, testing, measuring, and optimizing what works—and what doesn't—has become the cornerstone of my approach.

My life's work and attention are devoted to the concepts shared in this book. I've invested the requisite ten-thousand-plus hours to become an authority on this subject. I can promise you this: if you read this book with intention, you will gain insight into how companies create incredible breakthroughs that once seemed impossible.

You'll see how homegrown companies become world-renowned; how small businesses shift to big thinking, large enterprises; and how organizations scale with healthy, high-performing teams.

One of the most significant challenges faced in my career is building a team from hundreds to thousands while maintaining the integrity of the culture.

This book offers proven solutions that grow with you, wherever you are, whatever your next step.

- Leading a small team and aiming to reach ten? You'll find exactly what you need.
- Ready to double your team from ten to twenty? We can get there, together.
- Looking to 10X your impact from twenty to two hundred? This framework was built for scale.

- Already leading two thousand and now tasked with reaching twenty thousand globally? The principles in these pages still hold true.

Whether you're just starting out or navigating the complexity of global operations, **The E3 Effect** meets you where you are and helps you lead what's next.

And if you're part of a large-scale organization searching for tested, but still untapped, insights that drive real outcomes, you're in the right place.

The Power of Vision

To begin, I want to share a story about my family. (My wife is Dawn, and my son is Aston.) When Aston was ten, I attended a training course called *The 4 Disciplines of Execution* (4DX). It's about how to drive exceptional results with fully engaged teams that buy into the team goals. Newly certified in 4DX, I was energized when I left that session. At home, I immediately shared my new insight with my family, as I always do when encountering something that piques my interest. I immediately wanted to put it into action to see if it was feasible.

As a homeschooling family who prioritized travel as part of our approach, Dawn ran point given her experience as a former teacher. The process of homeschooling is, in a way, like business: It's centered around goals and objectives, adjustments to the plan, and reframing ideas to generate intended actions. I observed homeschooling as a methodology, a workflow, and realized it needed purpose and direction.

One of the objectives created with Dawn—and later with Aston—was that he learn a second language. It was important that he experience success through the development of this skill. He chose Spanish.

For the 4DX results, we needed a goal. The goal we created as a family was for him to be able to speak conversationally for thirty minutes with someone fluent in Spanish. If that person confirmed Aston was conversational, we would take him on a trip to any Spanish-speaking country of his choosing.

One part of 4DX involves active engagement in creating a board to measure success. We decided to make a poster. We all worked together as a team to create it, and it included measurable lead and lag indicators, with weekly tracking toward the goal.

As part of the process, we wanted to make it fun and personalized. We went to the craft store, and he picked out a poster board, markers, and star stickers. They even had decorations featuring the names of major cities around the world. He selected a few of those.

When we came home, the map of Spain went on the poster board, and he drew a line imagining a trip he was excited about. He said, "This is where I want to go." He was in.

As life happens, he studied Spanish but didn't make quick progress. Still, we used the 4DX board, discussed it weekly, and maintained the routine for several months. Then, like many things, our focus faded.

What we *did* do, though, was leave the board—that vision—up on the wall, in a spot where he would subconsciously see it every day. It remained there throughout high school.

During the college application process, studying international relations abroad called to him. He applied to several universities outside of the U.S., one of which was IE University in Madrid, with a secondary campus in a historic town to the north where he would begin his studies. At some point, while looking over the poster board, we realized something: He had seen the decoration labeled "Madrid" and the line leading to a dot every day. That little dot? It was Segovia.

Subconsciously, he had been moving toward Madrid and Segovia his entire youth, all through his schooling years, and ultimately chose a university without initially realizing it had a campus right where his vision had placed him all those years ago.

Vision is a critical component woven into many aspects of this book. I share that story because sometimes things happen subconsciously and unconsciously—if you allow the idea to develop. Incredible things can happen if you create an idea, enable it, and let it linger without limiting thoughts.

A central theme and what this book is exponentially about is leveling up employee performance through the **E3 Performance Rubric**:

Enable, Empower, Endeavor.

I wish you success on your own journey. This book is a guide, a sherpa, to support you in reaching the highest level of success if you choose to take a proven path.

When you reach the end, your vision will be broader; your ability to connect, grow, and engage with your team, as well as generate results, will be stronger; your speed to results will be significantly faster. You will develop the skills to work smarter, not harder.

PHASE 1: ENABLE

Foundation for Beyond Possible

CHAPTER 1

DEFINING CULTURE

Measure what matters. Yes, that includes culture.

Why Culture Still Feels So Hard to Define

Culture. We talk about it constantly in leadership conversations, yet it often remains vague, abstract, or misunderstood. We know it when it's there—and we certainly know when it's missing. But what is it, really?

Is it the tone in a meeting? The attitude of the team? The behavior when no one's watching?

The truth is, culture is not soft. It's not fluffy. It's the garden or ecosystem from which performance grows—or withers. And while it may seem intangible, it can be observed, shaped, measured, and grown.

But before we can do any of that, we need to define it clearly.

What Is Culture?

Anthropologist Clifford Geertz once described culture as "webs of significance" that humans themselves have spun. In simple terms, culture is the shared meaning we assign to our experiences, behaviors, and values. It shapes how we interpret situations, make decisions, respond to one another, and pursue goals.

In an organizational context, culture is the invisible force that binds a group of individuals together toward a collective mission greater than themselves. It is not something imposed—it is something cultivated. And like any living system, its health depends on the environment in which it grows.

Culture shows up in the unspoken agreements between teammates. It lives in how people respond to pressure, how trust is extended, how accountability is upheld, and how leaders engage with those around them. It's observed in the rhythm, the pulse, and the energy of your team.

And while culture can feel hard to define, I've found that it becomes much more tangible when broken down into its essential elements.

The Core Components of Culture

Over the years, I've studied, observed, and led teams through change across industries—from Fortune 500s to start-ups. And I've come to identify seven key elements that fundamentally shape and sustain culture. These aren't abstract ideas; they're the real, operational components that you'll see come up again and again in high-performing teams:

Engagement – The energy and attention people give to their work.

Support – The sense of being backed, valued, and seen by leadership and peers.

Enabling Others – Actively creating opportunities for people to grow and succeed.

Hope – Belief in a better future, even in the face of challenges.

Change – How a team relates to transformation, ambiguity, and evolution.

Trust – The invisible currency that powers communication and collaboration.

Vision – A shared picture of success that gives purpose to action.

Each of these components plays a role in your culture. Together, they form the web—the ecosystem, imagined as a garden—that determines how your people show up and what they believe is possible.

If culture is a shared system of learned beliefs, behaviors, values, and symbolic meanings that binds a group of individuals toward a collective mission greater than themselves, when does it form? When *people willingly look beyond their differences to discover the synergy among them,* leveraging focus, determination, work ethic, and mutual respect to achieve extraordinary outcomes.

More than operational habits or surface behaviors, *culture is the invisible force*—what Clifford Geertz called "webs of significance"—that gives meaning to a group's actions. These symbolic structures shape how individuals interpret challenges, align their efforts, and pursue purpose together.

Why Culture Matters in High-Performing Teams

When optimized, culture becomes the connective tissue that transforms a disparate group into a high-performing unit capable of moving a business or cause toward bold, unified progress.

Once we understand culture not just as a behavior, but as an ecosystem, the shared system of meaning, belief, and purpose that binds people together, we realize: **culture isn't imposed—it's cultivated.** And like any ecosystem, its strength depends on the conditions we create. If we want our people to align, to believe, and to contribute at their best, then culture must begin with the environment. The foundation of every high-performing culture is a space where people feel safe, seen, challenged, and supported. **It starts with creating an environment where people can thrive.**

Is something like this even measurable? Culture is an experience that is present or not. It's a particular vibe when you walk into a room. Whether joining a call or entering a space, a vibrant mood, palpable connection, or engagement with the work is evident. It is. This chapter will help answer this question for you.

WIIFM: What's In It For Me?

The first thing to focus on is authentic connection. What's essential to the team members, to the company, and to the individuals doing the work? What do they value?

For example, I love my family, mountain biking, travel, and being outside in nature. So it's important to me that I have time to travel, be with my family, and experience mountain biking. But when I'm in the office or at work, I want to be highly focused and make a difference. When my leader knows that about me, they can engage and connect in a way that aligns my work with a much larger goal—the "why" I am working and the radio station everyone listens to: WIIFM—What's In It For Me. When a leader doesn't take the time to get to know you, they miss opportunities to connect and engage with your WIIFM. Then, the work becomes dissociated from your personal objectives. When an individual's need isn't linked to the "why" behind their working and the "how" they'll achieve their WIIFM, it's difficult to connect with the job.

Let's Talk About Engagement

If you don't take the time to engage and get to know your team, you won't be able to detect changes or signs of distress. That's a key point. I used the word "**engage**" intentionally.

An engaged leader identifies when behaviors change—when a department, a team, or an individual shifts their behavior. It's everything to recognize those moments. I've come to call these "moments of disengagement." I'll give a quick example here.

IN PRACTICE: There was a time when I had a team member—let's call him Jamie—who was in management and was one of the most selfless, giving individuals I've known. If someone had a flat tire or needed a battery jump, he would be the first to raise his hand and say, "Hey, I'm coming out to help you." If someone had a complex work issue, he was always the first to jump in.

Then, one day, a team member had a flat tire, and Jamie didn't raise his hand. He didn't go outside. He didn't offer to help. At first, I disregarded the moment. I thought, *Well, maybe he's just busy*. I let it go, but I made a mental note of it. A few other events occurred. In one case, a peer needed help, and Jamie wasn't eager to jump in.

> This is a moment in which **culture is measurable**: Jamie went from being engaged with his team to being disengaged. He was no longer participating in the culture.

One morning, when Jamie arrived, I invited him to lunch.

I said, "I'd just love to catch up with you," which was honest and straightforward. So we scheduled it.

In the car, on the way, I wasted no time. I said, "Jamie, do you mind if I ask a question? If I'm off base, just tell me, and I'll drop it."

He agreed. I continued: "Well, my observation is that in the past, when a team member needed support, you were always the first to jump in. Whether it was on a personal level, a professional level, or for a customer, you've always been that person for the team. I'm just not seeing it as often. I'm just curious: Is anything going on that might explain what I'd describe as a level of ***disengagement*** at times?"

Jamie looked at me and said, "Is it that obvious?"

I was genuinely interested in Jamie and continued, "Yes, but I want to check in—because perception isn't always the truth."

He shared, "My fiancée and I are saving to buy our first home. We're getting married and planning to have a baby soon after that. So I need to make more money. At night, I've been doing gig work—Uber Eats, Uber, Lyft, that kind of thing. My fiancée comes with me, so we're together, but I've been staying up quite late. I'm coming in tired, and that's probably what you're seeing."

I said, "First—congratulations on all these great things happening in your life! I want to support you through these big milestones. And I'd also love to get the best out of you while you're here. Can we talk about how we might be able to do that?"

Jamie said, "Daniel, I would love that. I really enjoy the team and the work we do, but I just need to make more money."

How many people have said that before? *I just need to make more money.*

While I couldn't guarantee he'd make more money, I worked with him to identify ways he could make a bigger impact at the organization—play a bigger game—that might open the door to new opportunities. And he stepped up in a big way.

After some time had passed, he earned a promotion. We created a new role that didn't previously exist in the organization. He added so much value that he was able to earn sufficient income to stop the evening gig work.

We were fortunate to have Jamie's full energy and support once again. Engaged people stick around.

Every team member has a personal "why" behind showing up—and it's not simply a paycheck. When leaders take the time to understand the "why," they unlock deeper motivation and connection. Culture becomes real when personal goals and organizational purpose align. That's when people stop checking boxes and start showing up fully.

The Fundamentals of Culture

What are the **fundamentals of culture**? They're **measurable**. As I mentioned earlier, many people say culture is soft, it's fuzzy, it's just something you know when it's right or when it's not. I say yes to all of that, and I also say: Culture is objective and tangible. Throughout this chapter, we lay out multiple ways culture can be observed and, therefore, measured. When we close out, look for a quick checklist to be sure you didn't miss one.

We can establish measurements to assess and ensure a healthy culture. This can be purposeful and conscious, something you ***think deeply*** about.

Imagine a garden that hasn't been tended in some time. It's probably not fruitful. The longer it has been neglected, the more weed-choked and barren the starting point will be.

Take a look and ask yourself: What are the elements of my culture? A healthy culture requires removing everything that stands in the way. It won't happen overnight, but the results are worth the effort.

As we design the garden of an organization, we begin with the nutrients in the soil. That is the foundation of your leadership. The seeds you choose are your people, and how you align them with your vision determines where, when, and how to plant them. Water generously with development opportunities, and strategically position the sunlight for growth and enablement. Culture blooms. ***The E³ Effect*** has produced a world-class team. The goal of all this is a healthy and vibrant garden that yields the best of whatever your organization seeks to produce.

This process takes time, and you must continually communicate what you're doing, why you're doing it, and why it feels different. Over time, something important will happen: some people won't be a fit for this garden. They might choose a different path. They may say, "This garden is not for me."

This is a natural part of the process. Upcoming phases and chapters will delve more deeply into each of the garden elements as they relate to ***The E3 Effect*** methodology.

What Engagement Reveals About Role Fit

When a team member stops engaging, it's often a sign that their role no longer aligns with their strengths, goals, or motivation. By measuring those moments, you give yourself a chance to catch the disconnect early, before it turns into performance issues or quiet quitting.

Making sure someone is in the right role starts with paying attention to how often—and how meaningfully—they engage with you and others. That's why I always recommend asking yourself: how often are you checking in, connecting, and offering support? The frequency and quality of those touchpoints can reveal a lot. If engagement drops, it might not be about effort—it might be about fit.

That's something you can measure. Even a simple, "Good morning! I'm so glad you're here. Let me know how I can support you," counts. Over time, those moments tell you everything.

Help vs. Support

I don't use the word "**help**"—I use "**support**." "**Help**" is a perfectly fine word, and many people will continue to use it even after reading this. But "**help**" can have a negative connotation. If I help you, it implies you're in a place of weakness, and I'm here to get you to the next place. I use "support" because support lifts people. The word "**support**," by its nature, raises someone and acknowledges that they are fully capable of achieving or completing the task at hand. It's a nuance. It's contextual. That's just one way I'm very purposeful about culture.

Pathways for Idea-Sharing

Another measurement is: Is there a way for people to share ideas? As a rule, you can expect that team members will generate ideas—some are amazing and some don't serve the larger purpose. Ask yourself: Is there a clear path to **share ideas**? Do you have a tracking system—an **existence system**—for capturing ideas? Where are they being recorded so they exist in a useful way?

IN PRACTICE: For example, one of the questions I ask when I'm **guiding** team members to think creatively, especially those who struggle to come up with ideas or need a bit more comfort, is this: What's working well? What's not working well? What's working, but not as well as it could be?

And then I get interested. I pay close attention, with my eyes on them, my heart turned toward theirs, and my full attention focused. They are interesting, and what they have to share interests me. This creates a safe space for them to share their ideas freely.

After asking those questions, I continue by saying, "I'm curious about your reaction to those questions. What's there for you?" And then, I stop talking and listen. I give them space to think and respond. That enables and empowers them to engage and be innovative.

Enabling vs. Enforcing

A strong leader looks to **enable**, not **enforce.** To be clear, I acknowledge that there are situations where critical or urgent matters must be handled firmly, so this isn't an absolute statement. Yet, I've failed enough to realize that creating a healthy culture where high-performing teams can thrive means using force only as a last resort.

Ask yourself, how do you influence and achieve healthy results? How do you move things forward, especially when they require change and the team isn't comfortable or ready?

The first thing to ask is: Have you set up the team to be prepared? Have you openly and candidly shared with them what's happening within the organization? Have you given them space to hear, process, and ask questions? That way, when you come to them with a significant change, they have some context. But if this is the first time they're hearing about a substantial shift—without preparing the garden soil properly—they'll most likely push back.

So, how do you avoid resistance? One way is to ask another leader you respect how they de-risk before giving a new direction. How can you prepare the team?

For example, I might approach a team, a department, a company, or even an individual and start with, "I have an unreasonable request." This is disarming. I'm immediately acknowledging that what I'm about to ask may seem beyond reason. It provides people with space to ask questions, express concerns, and engage in an open dialogue to gain clarity.

CONVERSATION PLAYBOOK:

Begin with: " How is your day going so far? Is this a good time to talk?"

If I'm interrupting work: "Are you in the right headspace for this conversation?"

Then: "I have an unreasonable ask."

If they agree to the meeting: "I need support to make this happen. And here's the deal: No is not an option for us.

That's because the company has a strategic initiative, and our team directly impacts how that initiative goes. We're here to enable the company to be successful, which takes care of our customers, creates job stability, supports you, and opens the door for you to grow and develop in your career if we do this right together."

Use phrases like: "I call for everyone's engagement."

Then we figure out what they need to accept and engage. It's not the team member's or the team's job to determine that on their own—we work together to identify what's needed to accept and engage in the task.

It might be reasonable; it might be unreasonable—but it's change. It's innovation. It's new.

Put yourself in their shoes. What would you want to hear to truly understand and buy into what needs to be done for the organization? And if you have trouble with that, it's an established best practice to ask a few trusted people on the team before having the larger meeting, especially if it's a big group. Try your messaging with a few people, be curious about their reactions, and listen to their feedback.

Creating Hope

As a leader, your job is to create hope, especially when no one else sees a way forward. That may not come naturally at first. It didn't for me.

There was a quarter when we had just lost a major client, revenue was falling short, and the team felt the weight of it all. Morale dipped. People started whispering about layoffs. One of my team members came to me and said, "The team is in despair. We're struggling."

Then they asked the question you will never forget: "How are you going to help us?"

Maybe you've been there, doing everything you can behind the scenes. I shared what I was working on, the feedback I was hearing, the actions I was taking. I was transparent and honest. I told them, "We're going after the problem. I just don't know how it's going to end yet."

They paused and said, "There's no hope in that. We're going to stay in despair."

That moment shifted everything for me. You can be honest—but without a vision, honesty can feel hollow. As a leader, you're not just there to solve problems. You're there to create belief. To build an environment where people feel seen, supported, and inspired to believe that something better is possible—even before the path is clear.

Your team doesn't just need answers. They need to believe again.

So how do you create hope? How do you lead with positivity, especially when things feel uncertain?

Take something as difficult as layoffs. How do you reassure the team members who remain? You do it with clarity, honesty, and specific language that they sense they can trust and rely on. Give them a concrete base—words that don't just inform, but also restore a sense of direction and stability.

CONVERSATION PLAYBOOK:

Begin with: "Good morning, everyone. Thanks for taking the time to be here. The organization is focused on scaling to support a larger customer base. There have been learnings that require us to take a step back in order to move forward."

Explain your position: "Here's what I know. Here's what I don't know. One thing I cannot commit to is that your job is safe or that it will be here in the long term. I don't even know that for myself. I'd be lying otherwise. Here's what I can say: We can do everything we need to do to ensure the health of the organization, and be the team, the department, the group that stands out as taking the lowest effort to get results from, the easiest to work with, and the highest performing. That assures us of success. And if we are impacted, it prepares us for what's next. It's an opportunity to be real, to foster communication, and to build trust."

Measuring Change

What's another measurement you can put in place? Leaders can conduct follow-ups on a weekly, monthly, or quarterly basis.

What's new? Is it low-impact, medium-impact, or high-impact? What about your parking lot ideas? Instead of ignoring them or letting them sit in silence when someone offers an idea you're not ready to entertain or one that's already been considered and set aside, create a system for tracking them.

One thing I've done in the past is use tools such as Trello, Jira, and Monday.com—basically Kanban-style boards. I've worked with team members to create columns like: **New**, **Low-Impact**, **Medium-Impact**, **High-Impact**, **Parking Lot**, and **Won't Do**.

Team members can submit ideas at any time, similar to submitting tickets or cases. When they submit an idea, it will appear in the **New** column.

Throughout the week or month—whatever cadence you choose— meet with a subset of the team or the whole team, depending on the size and dynamics. Rotate members regularly. Together, determine if the idea is low-, medium-, or high-impact. Low-impact ideas could add value, like improving team members' quality of life at work.

Over time, the categorized lists within the **Kanban board** are implemented. With that, determine how many high-impact items can be realistically executed. Every company has a pace of change and inherent sprint durations.

Consider yours, and plan improvements accordingly; one high-impact item in a cycle may be possible, two medium-impact, or three low-impact projects.

Strategize with the team to select the next focus with the most significant value. Choices do not have to be unanimous. The objective is the engagement.

And when they're engaged, they trust. They know there's a process. They know they have a voice. They know their ideas are considered.

Building Trust

As billionaire Warren Buffett said, "It takes twenty years to build a reputation and five minutes to ruin it. If you think about that, you'll do things differently." As leaders, one way we put nutrients in our soil is to intentionally build our reputation, not only for ourselves but also for the organization we work within, and for the individual team members we trust.

Your reputation is directly correlated to the level of trust present in your team. It might be a controversial idea, but trust is measurable. This trust is observable, not manipulative. The mechanism for measuring trust is literally counting who promotes the culture and who detracts from it. As the flowers show up in the garden, they are unmistakable. They bring color, joy, and indicate a healthy space. The same can be said for the detractors.

Creating a North Star

Company missions could be broad and organization-wide or department-focused. Depending on the size of the department and the teams within it, the mission could even be team-specific. When all of these missions align, a **shared mission** emerges, giving the team a common purpose, which can generate hope even when things seem hopeless.

When a team has a shared purpose, the business has an end goal. It has a time-based strategic objective. Your team's purpose gives direction. It creates hope that you can reach that goal—you just need to figure out how. When a team is aligned, you start working smarter, not harder.

Working smarter helps generate a healthy culture. Your job as a leader is to guide the team to develop into a cohesive unit. Think of it like a rowing team, with the coxswain in the back calling out the rhythm. As a leader, you're that person. You need to protect your people, guide them, help them understand the cadence of rowing, and make sure everyone knows the direction we're heading.

Culture is a mindset. Most companies have a **mission and vision statement**. If they don't, that's an opportunity to unite everyone around a common purpose and create one. Even if the company doesn't have a clear mission or vision, you can still create one for your team. As a leader, do you have a mission that aligns with your direct leader's mission? Does it connect to the broader vision of the organization?

Then, the question becomes: Is that mission communicated? Is it shared regularly? For example,

I stepped into a fast-growing healthcare company that was deeply committed to its mission. But inside, cross-functional partnership was fractured, especially between the call center and other departments. The service center operated almost like a separate entity rather than an integrated part of the organization. Metrics didn't align with enterprise goals, accountability was inconsistent, and the absence of structure created a "management by chaos" culture. If you've ever led in that kind of environment, you know how hard it is to gain traction. A full transformation was needed—not just in systems and processes, but in mindset, alignment, and culture.

To begin that transformation, I deployed a **Listening Roadshow**.

Listening Roadshow: Involves interviewing leaders from every department across the enterprise. Listen for what matters most with respect to their expectations of their team and yours. Key takeaways involve insights on how they perceive your department in relation to theirs—across roles, responsibilities, measures, and perspectives.

At some point in this process, breakthrough insights emerged, and that's when I knew we didn't just need alignment—we needed a North Star.

From those conversations, common themes stood out that became the foundation of our North Star document: a set of guiding principles tied directly to the mission, and built to align culture with execution.

A **North Star principle** is the shared goal that keeps your team grounded in what matters most. It guides decisions and actions by tying your work directly to the company's mission—and your team's role in fulfilling it.

Most of my career has been in customer experience and other service-oriented roles. One leader described what she wanted from our call center in a particular way. She said, "We want a patient to experience a warm hug when they call in." That simple statement became the basis for our North Star principle: "serve warmly."

Another common expectation is around execution—doing the work accurately and efficiently, even as the company scaled. That gave rise to another principle: "executional excellence."

Finally, we recognized that continuous improvement and innovation were essential, particularly given the company's rapid growth. Staying where we were wasn't an option; we had to stay ahead of growth. That inspired our third principle: "inspirational innovation."

These principles came from somewhere—I didn't just make them up. *Serve warmly* had a story behind it. That story gave it meaning. That meaning built trust. And that trust gave the principle staying power over time. These weren't just words on a poster—they became the lens through which we made decisions, coached teams, hired leaders, and aligned our daily operations to the mission we all believed in.

Eventually, everything and everyone started to align with those **North Star principles**. That's what a North Star does—it re-centers the work around purpose and gives every person on the team a reason to keep moving forward together.

Culture is everything. Without the nutrients in the soil, the seeds you plant won't grow. Without the nourishment of the water of development, culture withers. When these fall into place, **hard things become possible, and the right things get easier to do.**

1.1 TAKE ACTION: North Star Worksheet—Define What You Stand For

This exercise will help you clarify what your team should be known for—and how those ideas show up (or don't) in daily work. Use it for personal reflection or to guide a meaningful conversation with your team and key cross-functional partners.

Step 1: Reflect

What are three qualities, principles, or experiences you want your team to generate—internally and externally?

Ask yourself:

- What do we want to be known for?
- What do others count on us for?
- What's limiting our performance—or holding us back from delivering at our best?

Step 2: Align

Now consider whether your current behaviors, metrics, and communication reflect those principles. For each one, ask yourself:

- Are our daily actions aligned with this?
- Where are we strong?
- What needs to shift?

Step 3: Activate

Pick one principle and take one small action this week to bring it to life. It might be how you shape strategic priorities, set team-wide or organizational expectations, or model key behaviors for your senior leaders to reinforce.

Ask yourself:

- Which principle will I act on first?
- What's one thing I can do this week to model it?

Step 4: Expand Your Lens

Don't stop with your own team. Reach out to cross-functional partners and ask:

- "What do you count on our team for?"
- "What would you say we're known for?"

Then reflect:

- Do their answers match what we think about ourselves?
- Are we delivering on what others need from us?

Use what you learn to refine your principles—and to build stronger alignment and trust across teams.

Step 5: Plan Forward

Develop a **3-month action plan** to define, socialize with your leaders, and put into practice your North Star principles. Be sure to define specific goals, outline key steps, and identify measurable outcomes so progress is visible and sustainable.

Culture alone isn't enough. Once the foundation is in place, you need a clear picture of what winning (success) looks like—and how to repeat it. Our goal is to create a **flywheel effect** of winning: a momentum-building loop where clear success factors and small wins compound into sustainable performance. That's what the next chapter will support: defining success and mapping out the milestones to achieve it, together.

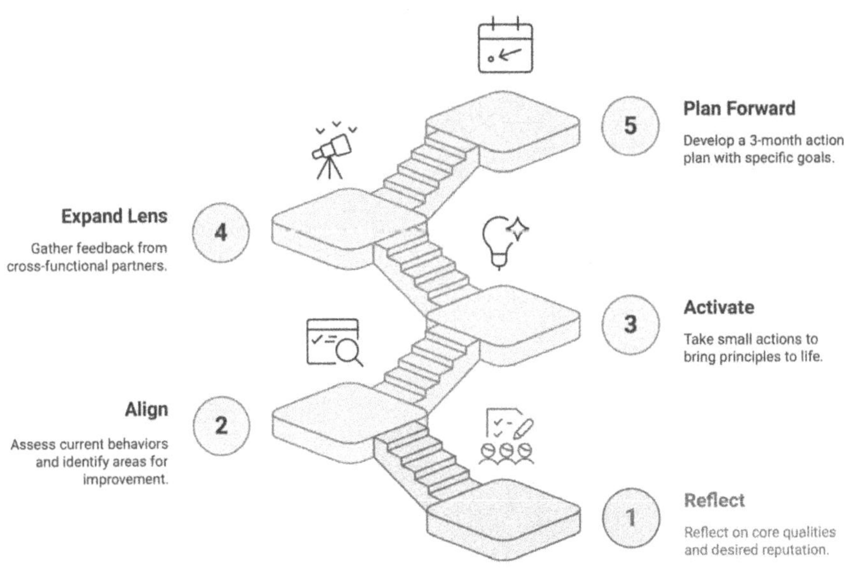

The flywheel effect starts with small wins—each success or milestone achieved adds velocity. As that potential builds, the wins get bigger, and the goals get bolder. With every objective met, your team earns confidence, and with it, the belief that bigger goals are within reach. Your role is to make those wins intentional and repeatable, so progress becomes self-sustaining.

Quick Check: Have you determined the various ways culture can be measured?

- What nutrients have you added to your soil?
- How much engagement is present?
- What is your weed count?
- Are you meeting your metrics?
- How many flowers do you observe?
- Are there natural rains and intentional watering of your seeds?

CHAPTER 2

DEFINING SUCCESS

What got you here won't get you there.

Success Is Not an Accident

Your efforts have brought you a long way, but here's the truth: what got you here won't necessarily get you to the next level. Everybody wants success, yet few have spelled it out in clear, actionable terms.

Success isn't a buzzword—it's a pattern of behaviors that produce results. In this chapter, we'll break down what success looks like in action through the E3 method, starting with clear Critical Success Factors (CSFs) and mapping them to measurable milestones that turn vision into motion.

Critical Success Factors vs. Milestones

At the outset, you might ask: "Aren't milestones the same as critical success factors?" They're connected, but they are not identical.

Critical Success Factors (CSFs) are the foundation. These are the essential conditions that must be in place for success to happen. Think of them as the groundwork—the elements that sustain long-term achievement. They answer the "why" behind your operations. For example, for a customer service role, a critical success factor might be ensuring every interaction meets a baseline of exceptional service and alignment with your North Star principles.

Milestones, on the other hand, are the markers along the journey. They take the foundational CSFs and break them down into achievable, trackable steps. Milestones answer the "how and when" of progress. They're the day-to-day responsibilities and targets that demonstrate you're moving toward the big picture. In our example, milestones for a member coordinator might include serving as the primary point of contact, addressing member concerns promptly, and even conducting root cause analyses.

By defining both, you make it clear that success is built on foundational elements (CSFs) that then shape measurable actions (milestones). This clarity is what transforms a lofty vision into something tangible.

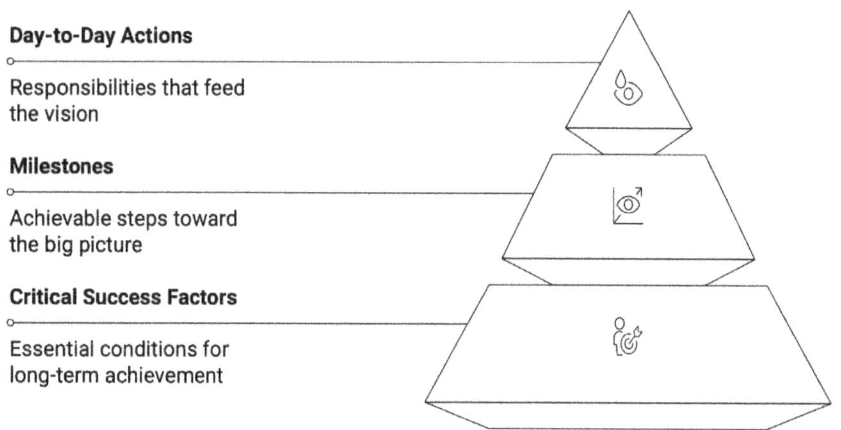

Everybody chases success, but have you actually spelled it out? The **E3 Method** calls for defining **critical success factors**, which then develop into **milestones** that call for aligned **day-to-day actions**. You may wonder: aren't milestones the same as critical success factors? No—critical success factors precede milestones. And day-to-day responsibilities are the nutrients that feed your ***vision***.

These are not overnight changes and are not supposed to be. Articulating the elements makes all the difference. Let's look at an example in action.

Take a job description for a member coordinator handling back office tasks and answering calls. They're expected to provide exceptional service aligned with your **North Star Principles**; the tactical guide for the organization.

Consider that as a leader, your focus is the high-level vision, yet your people's priority, before they become a team, is their day-to-day. Knowing this, you design the job description that clearly illustrates how their responsibilities naturally tie to the bigger picture. The more you make that real for them, the easier their path to engagement.

Think about when *you* were last interviewed. You want to know: what will a day in your life be like? How will you know you are being successful, and when? In the day-to-day responsibilities section for this role, it could include serving as the primary point of contact, fostering relationships, addressing concerns and issues, ensuring members derive maximum value from their membership, resolving issues promptly, conducting root cause analyses, upholding the core values in every interaction, and striving for excellence in outcomes.

Those are just some examples in the customer service space. If it's a finance, marketing, sales, or operations role, the tasks might be different, but they still follow the same thought process.

For example, in one organization, I deployed a six-month, milestone-based success timeline. This served as a blueprint for how role-based expectations are structured and measured over time. While the exact milestones will vary by position, the underlying framework—anchored in progression, clarity, and impact—remains consistent.

The member coordinator role included five key milestones, tracked over time, giving us insight into both individual performance and the effectiveness of our onboarding and support systems.

The key is how you communicate throughout the journey—not just setting the bar, but walking alongside them through it. We'll explore practical strategies for coaching, feedback, and celebrating progress so that defining success becomes more than words on a page.

These five milestones serve as a roadmap for professional growth and performance in the member coordinator role (or any similar role). While timelines may vary, the progression helps ensure employees are set up for success, and leaders know how to support them

The Five Milestones

- **Milestone 1: Gain credibility by mastering your company's offerings and understanding your stakeholders' needs**. Get to know the structural elements of the company, who your stakeholders are, and why they need what they need from you.

- **Milestone 2: Seamlessly integrate into your team and confidently manage your routine tasks.** Are they a team player? Are they easy to work with? That starts to tell them who we want them to be. Can they handle their everyday work? And can they do it with confidence? Can they do it well?

- **Milestone 3: Handle complex issues independently while contributing to service improvements.** So now they're handling the routine tasks confidently, but when they have a complex problem or task, can they handle it independently? Are they contributing to improving the overall service the team develops and delivers? Are they part of improving it?

- **Milestone 4: Managing a growing portfolio—this is productivity, however you define the metric.** They successfully manage increasing productivity and achieve an expert level within the role.

- **Milestone 5: Demonstrate proactive engagement, collaboration, and problem-solving skills while preparing for advancement.** This is where it all comes together. Now, you might ask, why would you include "preparing for advancement"? Forward thinking is one way to water your seeds with development.

Clear, well-defined expectations are essential when managing a new team member, or even a seasoned one, without clear goals. When a team member struggles or needs clarification, one effective approach is to develop a milestone-based framework and walk them through it. This process supports their growth and simplifies management by establishing expectations upfront.

These milestones should be treated as a dynamic, evolving document. Business needs change, and the framework should reflect that flexibility. I make a point of sitting down with my direct reports—and sometimes with their team members as well—to go through each item in the document. I want them to know I am fully committed to this process, just as I expect them to be. It's not about issuing directives from above; it's about building mutual trust and follow-through. Progressing through the milestones produces measurable outcomes. It demonstrates care, connection, and clarity of purpose.

Let's take a closer look at the six-month timeframe, keeping in mind that timelines will vary depending on the role; some may take just a few weeks or months, while others might require up to a year or more. For the specific role I have in mind, six months is typically the time it takes to move through all the key milestones. I introduce this timeline to the new hire as part of their onboarding, the first time we meet.

IN PRACTICE: I explain that, on average, it takes six months to complete the process. Some have achieved it in as little as three months, and one person even completed it in two. Others have needed up to nine. If we're approaching the eleven- or twelve-month mark, however, that usually calls for a different kind of conversation.

Throughout the process, we track progress together. The goal is for the new hire to always know exactly where they stand in relation to expectations. I ask them to keep a copy of the document so they can mark their progress, using highlights, bold text, or strikethroughs as needed.

For each milestone, I encourage them to document when they completed each specific criterion. This helps them internalize their responsibilities and take ownership of their role. The goal is not to rely on the leader to pull them forward, but to empower them to drive their progress.

This approach is about working smarter. When milestones are tracked and documented in this way, one-on-ones, quarterly check-ins, and annual reviews become more meaningful and efficient. The team member can come prepared, saying, "Here's where I see myself. Here's what I've accomplished." In turn, the manager can respond clearly: "You excelled in this area—great job. This other one still needs attention. Keep working on it." These conversations become easier, more objective, and insanely productive.

It's not uncommon for someone to move ahead on milestones out of order—for example, completing a step from Milestone 3 while still working through Milestone 1. That flexibility can work, depending on the situation. However, it's essential to recognize when skipping ahead can cause problems.

At one company, we hired a technically skilled individual for a high-level support team that offered white-glove service to a demanding client base. By immediately applying their advanced technical knowledge, solving complex issues, Milestones 3 and 4 were essentially bypassed. In doing so, foundational steps from Milestone 1, such as understanding the company's mission, goals, and working method, were overlooked. Essential parts of

Milestone 2, team integration and collaboration, were also skipped. As a result, despite technical competence, overall performance and impact were compromised.

It showed up this way: solutions were reached through incorrect conclusions, both in how they approached the issue and in the resolutions proposed. The root of the problem was clear: skipping over foundational development steps opened gaps for key pitfalls. These critical elements aren't intuitive unless they've been studied, internalized, and practiced. This experience underscores the importance of setting clear expectations and working through them collaboratively.

In short, the milestone framework provides structure, fosters accountability, and supports both individual and organizational success when used thoughtfully and in sequence.

Leveraging Tools to Support Success

Let me share a more specific example of how defining success made a tangible difference with a recently promoted team member. The reporting structure was pretty simple: me, this leader, and the frontline team. For a brief period, one of the frontline team members reported directly to me.

During our one-on-one meetings, I noticed that she became emotional and ended up in tears roughly eighty percent of the time. Naturally, that's not the desired outcome for these conversations. I found myself confused and conflicted, so I checked in with her more directly.

She explained, "I'm sorry—I just get overwhelmed. I feel like I'm not doing things as well as they're supposed to be done."

I told her that I understood and respected her honesty. To better support her, we took a step back and decided to use a combination of tools—a new hire evaluation and a behavioral style assessment. My preferred tool is the

Predictive Index, though you may be more familiar with **DISC (Dominance, Influence, Steadiness, and Conscientiousness)**, **Myers-Briggs**, or others.

But there's a critical difference between simply administering these assessments and actively using the insights they provide.

When I reviewed her results, the issue became clear: Her style was highly black and white. Whenever I gave guidance that included nuance or flexibility—anything "gray"—she felt she didn't have enough information to execute at a high level. Even when she performed well, she often felt like she had failed simply because she hadn't followed a precise, linear path from start to finish.

That realization prompted a shift in my approach. I needed to provide her with clearer, more structured direction. But that created a dilemma: Most of our work isn't black and white.

So the question became: How do I reconcile that reality with her way of processing information? How do we work together within that tension?

IN PRACTICE: In our next one-on-one, I took a different approach. I said, "I've been thinking a lot about how we work together. Today, I'd like to set aside our usual agenda and revisit our Predictive Index profiles. Let's use this time to get to know each other better—both personally and through the lens of objective insights."

We had both reviewed our profiles previously and agreed they accurately reflected how we operate. To build trust, I went first. I shared the section from my profile that described how she could manage me, and I discussed my leadership style: how I think, make decisions, and what my management strategy looks like. I also offered a few personal insights about my behavior in the workplace. Then it was her turn. She shared how she works best and what she needs to thrive. By the end of that session, we had created a foundation of mutual understanding and trust.

That conversation felt like clearing weeds from a garden, making space, watering with development, and aligning the sunlight that allows you to have this tool to deploy. The dialogue about our Predictive Index results was just the beginning. Now it was time for flowers to grow and the culture to show up.

She was already familiar with the **Net Promoter Score** (NPS) system, where ratings of 9s and 10s are **Promoters**, 7s and 8s are **Passive**, and 1–6 are **Detractors**. Understanding that allowed us to co-create a framework. From that point on, at the start of every meeting, we'd begin with, "Tell me—where are you at, on a scale of 1 to 10?" She knew exactly what it meant. It became our code language.

> **NPS** is a survey metric that asks: How likely are you to recommend this? Scores sort into Promoters (9–10), Passives (7–8), and Detractors (0–6). The real value isn't just the number—but when it's asked in the member journey and what the comments reveal.

If she said, "I'm a 9," we both knew she was in a great place with work. There was nothing urgent to resolve—we could focus on moving forward.

If she said, "I'm a 7 or 8,"

I'd say, "Understood. Is there anything I can support you with?"

She'd respond yes or no. If yes, we'd use that meeting to focus on what I could do to make a difference.

If she said she was at 3, 4, or 5, it was a signal that something wasn't right. Either there was a breakdown in her understanding of the role, or she felt she couldn't complete the work at the level she expected from herself. We'd spend that meeting having conversations which led to follow-ups and action items, and many times, the action items landed with me, not her, because it's my job to clear the path for her to be successful. That's a peek into how milestones, success, and support coalesce.

Critical Success Factors

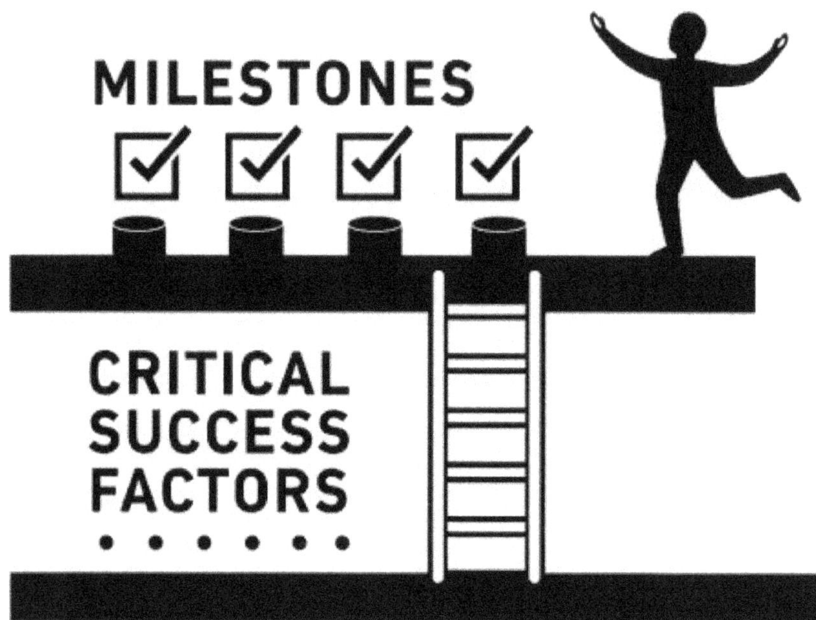

At the top of the chapter, we distinguished the relationship of critical success factors to milestones. Let's delve into the ones that will lead to the identified milestones in this member coordinator role:

- **Accountability**: Take complete ownership of both external concerns and internal responsibilities, ensuring consistent follow-through and resolution of issues. Solve the problem.

- **Integrity**: Provide accurate information and deliver the correct answer.

- **Urgency and Immediacy**: Respond quickly and effectively, providing timely and authentic communication that exceeds the expectations of time-pressed leaders. Build trust through reliable follow-up.

- **Relationships**: Build trusted, meaningful connections with customers and internal colleagues, fostering collaboration and loyalty through personal engagement.

- **Culture and Collaboration**: Align with company values while working closely with internal stakeholders to enhance service and drive long-term customer satisfaction. In some organizations, loyalty is often defined by customer retention.

When met, these purposefully translate into the milestones. In practice, the team member takes on responsibilities that contribute to key success factors and help achieve important milestones. One key distinction of the E3 method is to first determine these milestones, break down the critical success factors, and tie each into day-to-day work for your team. This is a top-down strategy effectuated using a bottom-up approach. It may be counterintuitive and take some practice until this skill is mastered.

Returning to the milestones for the role—building credibility, mastering offerings, understanding customer needs, handling routine tasks confidently, achieving expert-level support, and demonstrating collaboration with problem-solving skills—all are critically supported by what are now the core success factors. This is the essence of milestone design: identifying success factors, breaking each into actionable steps, and using those steps to create a structured pathway for a team.

Meeting milestones creates wins. When someone joins a new organization, one of their primary concerns is: Am I doing well enough? Am I on the right track? Milestones provide needed clarity around these questions. Including something as foundational as "understanding our customers' needs" gives direction and purpose.

Intentionally separate routine tasks (Milestone 2) from expert-level responsibilities (Milestone 4). This structure allows individuals to experience a sense of achievement as they progress.

It is essential to recognize and highlight progress, even within a single milestone. Each step forward contributes to momentum, confidence, and a strong sense of ownership.

Creating Measurable Outcomes

The framework of critical success factors and milestones can be applied to organizations of any size. The previous section focused on how they function at an individual level. The concepts are just as valuable at the team, departmental, organizational, and even enterprise levels. The primary difference lies in the scope of the outcomes and the scale of the impact.

But why does that matter to you, the leader, generating a garden with a winning team? Here's why. If that garden receives no sunlight, your efforts produce a smaller yield.

The E3 approach asserts that organizational support is like the sunlight to your team's growth and enablement. Positioning yourself well is another key nutrient in your leadership toolbox.

The higher the level within the organization, the greater the potential influence on overall success and alignment with strategic objectives. For this reason, businesses that define their critical success factors, **ideally through an annual planning process,** gain a competitive edge.

The E3 Effect calls upon organizations to start with the fundamental question: What do we want to accomplish in the year ahead? From there, a roadmap is created to guide the organization to its vision. Build your garden inside this larger one.

Once the roadmap is in place, it's translated into measurable outcomes. While metrics vary by organization and role, the five most commonly tracked include:

1. Revenue growth
2. Profitability
3. Customer retention
4. Net Promoter Score (NPS)
5. Customer Acquisition Cost (CAC).

Healthy organizations ensure that metrics align with the organization's goals and each department's unique focus.

IN PRACTICE: When applied at the organizational level, this process drives alignment. Consider a company that sets three clear goals for the year: Grow sales by twelve percent, reduce expenses by twenty percent, and maintain or improve the customer experience. With this clarity, each department can contribute in a way that aligns with its function and influence.

For example:

- **Human Resources** might focus on employee retention. Retaining talent reduces hiring costs, improves continuity, and increases expertise—all of which contribute to higher performance and cost efficiency. Attrition is expensive; reducing it is a strategic win.

- **Product teams** may ask how they can enhance their offerings to drive revenue or optimize processes for automation and efficiency, thereby reducing costs while multiplying value.

- **Service teams** provide valuable customer feedback, improving business intelligence, providing insights that catapult results to all three goals.

Understanding the big picture serves you as a leader and informs the decisions you make when you set your vision, choose your people, and define your critical success factors. When you tune into the partnership required to row in concert, not as individual departmental visions, but as one **cross-functional collaboration,** organizations get across the line. By identifying shared goals and departmental contributions, teams act as strategic partners rather than isolated units.

Within a Service Department, for example, there might be opportunities to reduce customer churn. Retaining customers means preserving revenue, depending on the business model, and contributing directly to organizational goals. Teams can then ask, "What strategies can we implement to improve retention?" What actions are within our control?

One proven method is to evaluate operational efficiency. Using tools like time-motion studies—common in call centers and manufacturing and rooted in **Lean Six Sigma** methodology—teams can assess workflows and identify bottlenecks. First, the workflow is mapped from start to finish. Then, the time required for each step is measured to identify which areas consume the most time.

> **Lean Six Sigma methodology** improves performance by reducing waste and variation. It blends Lean's speed with Six Sigma's precision to streamline workflows and boost quality. Common wastes include waiting, rework, overproduction, and unnecessary motion—each one slowing teams down and undermining results.

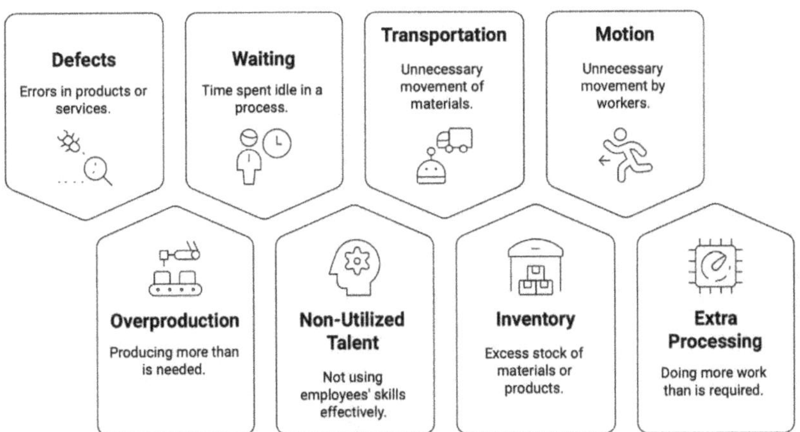

Let's take a real-world example: At one organization, customers were consistently frustrated by three minutes of "press one, press two" in an interactive voice response (IVR) system to reach a representative. Too many became lost or gave up. By analyzing the data and reworking the script, IVR navigation time was compressed to forty-five seconds.

Did that change impact customer retention? Absolutely. Shortening the window gave a better chance to serve—and retain—those customers. This is the value of defining critical success factors at every level of the organization: It promotes department and cross-functional alignment, encourages ownership, and equips teams to act intentionally. When paired with clear milestones, it creates a structure that enables individuals and departments to contribute meaningfully to long-term success.

2.1 TAKE ACTION: Let's take a Six Sigma example on the expense side in your garden. Pick a process or action that you know is causing unnecessary expenses. One of the most practical questions we can ask is: How can we reduce the time it takes to complete this task? Are there unnecessary delays between steps? Are we seeing recurring defects or errors that could be improved? If your answer is yes, then those are areas worth targeting. The focus should be on identifying what is within your control and acting upon it. From this analysis, we establish step goals: concrete, manageable improvements that move us forward. These serve as the foundation for setting aspirational goals, a key concept of **The E3 Effect**. Set a time to discuss this with your team, and add it to your existence system tool.

The underlying purpose of this approach is to help your people experience success. Your goal is to create a flywheel effect of winning, where **culture fuels performance** and **performance reinforces culture**. Let that be a key takeaway you carry forward.

When individuals and teams feel they're succeeding, when they experience clear, tangible wins, they become more confident. That confidence, in turn, motivates them to take on larger, more ambitious challenges.

On the other hand, when people feel stuck (confused, disconnected, or underperforming), it becomes difficult for them to envision what they're capable of achieving next. Momentum stalls. That's why creating early, achievable wins is crucial. It builds belief, fuels engagement, and lays the groundwork for success.

Before we can build this **culture of high performance**, we must bring the right seeds into the prepared soil. Hiring is not simply about evaluating talent—each step is an opportunity to demonstrate what it feels like to be part of this successful, supportive team. Speaking with candidates creates early moments where culture comes to life.

In the next chapter, I'll cover how I approach interviews—not just to assess talent, but to set the tone for the culture I am building.

The E3 Effect is exponential as it multiplies your current expertise (what got you here) with a few key tweaks that may have been hidden from your view. Pulling new knowledge towards you as a leader is like watering your garden, spurring your own growth (will get you there).

CHAPTER 3

INTERVIEWING

The best candidate on paper means nothing if they can't thrive with you.

You've probably sat through—or even led—dozens of interviews and yet still found yourself onboarding people who never quite fit. You've followed the templates, memorized the questions, and hoped that scoring grids would guarantee success. And yet, time and again, you've watched top talent turn away, not because they lacked skill, but because something vital was missing: a human connection from the very first moment.

In this chapter, you'll discover how to transform your interview process into a genuine conversation—one that both honors the candidate's experience and plants the seeds of your team's culture. You'll learn to open with compassion (not rhetoric), to tie every challenge to real work (not gimmicks), and to orchestrate each round as part of a seamless, collaborative dialogue.

Think of each interview question as an invitation: an invitation to reveal values, to share stories, and to imagine possibilities together. When you lead with that mindset, you don't just assess competence—you model the trust, transparency, and teamwork you want on day one.

Below, you'll find proven "in practice" examples and guiding principles to help you—and your future colleagues—conduct interviews that are consistent, purposeful, insightful, and, above all, human. Let's turn your hiring process into your strongest expression of leadership.

When I conduct interviews, I always begin with an intentional icebreaker—something to put the candidate at ease. Interviews are inherently stressful. As the interviewer, you can help alleviate that pressure and foster a productive, honest conversation. This practice also demonstrates to the interviewee how I lead teams in stressful moments: with compassion. Consciously or subconsciously, that matters. Even for candidates who don't appear nervous, establishing a human connection before diving into formal questions helps create a more open and collaborative atmosphere.

Lead with one of your strengths: I genuinely care about people. That care is the foundation of how I approach interviews. What's yours?

IN PRACTICE: Here's how I typically begin: "Before we get started, Eli, I want to say that this is a selection process—for *you* as much as it is for us. You're here to determine whether this is the right place for you, and we're here to assess whether you're the right fit for the team." This framing tends to lower the stakes and shifts the tone from interrogation to conversation. It reinforces that this is a two-way process.

After establishing that, I continue: "And of course, it's also my responsibility to determine whether you're a good fit for us. So I'll be asking the questions I need to ask to get the information I need—and I hope you'll do the same. Ask what you need to know to decide whether this is the right place for you."

That moment often shifts the energy. The interview becomes more balanced, personal, and genuine. In my experience, many candidates haven't encountered this kind of approach before, and it can make a lasting impression. Many top performers on my team have later remarked on how different my approach was to them, how much they appreciated it, and how it influenced their decision to join the team.

That said, interviews should still include appropriate challenges. If a candidate is applying for a technical role (say, a developer or engineer), they should expect to demonstrate their expertise, whether through coding exercises, technical assessments, or case-based problem-solving. But those challenges must serve a purpose. Likewise, if a candidate is applying for a service role (say, a relationship manager or call center agent), they should expect to demonstrate values alignment, operational maturity and expertise, and cultural alignment (team fit).

My perspective is this: Don't make an interview difficult just for the sake of creating stress. The challenge should be directly tied to the real work of the role. That builds trust. When candidates understand why they're being tested in a particular way, they're more likely to feel respected and engaged. They can see that the process is designed with **intention** and **transparency**.

As leaders, it's not just your responsibility to conduct strong interviews—it's your responsibility to define and communicate what success looks like in both the hiring process and the role itself. That includes setting a high standard for interview quality, alignment with the role profile, and helping others do the same. Leadership requires developing others, and you can start watering your seeds at this moment—preparing involved current and future team members to conduct effective interviews themselves, including efficient coordination across multiple rounds.

Too often, candidates go through three or four interviews, or a **panel process**, and end up repeating the same information over and over. That adds no value for the candidate or the hiring team. Instead, strong organizations employ a **shared interview strategy**. Each interviewer is developed to build on the previous conversations, with notes and key takeaways shared in advance. This streamlines the process and demonstrates to the candidate that we are aligned, intentional, and collaborative. This fosters early buy-in. When candidates see that your process reflects your culture, values, and attention to detail, they begin to feel like a part of the team, even before they join.

Finally, incorporating personality or **value-based questions** can further deepen mutual understanding and support cultural alignment.

IN PRACTICE: Occasionally, I'll even bring in a lighthearted question from years past—something fun, like: "What kitchen appliance would you be? Or what superhero best represents you?" These types of questions may seem whimsical, but they often lead to unexpected insights and meaningful conversation. They encourage people to get creative and step outside their usual way of thinking. If they choose a refrigerator, spatula, or blender, then I get a more profound sense of their personality. I learn what's important to them and what they value.

Another approach I use during interviews involves the classic behavioral prompt: "Tell me about a time when…" These questions invite candidates to reflect on their past experiences and provide supporting examples. It's one thing to evaluate creativity, but it's another to assess how someone thinks through real-life challenges and applies judgment in dynamic situations.

Another strategy is to present a hypothetical scenario and explore how the candidate would navigate it. One that has proven exceptionally effective: The Party Scenario.

CONVERSATION PLAYBOOK:

Frame the scenario: "I'm going to walk you through a scenario. Please take a moment to listen, and feel free to ask questions if anything is unclear. Once I'm done, I'd like you to share your initial reaction and talk me through the actions you'd take—step by step."

Once the candidate understands the instructions: "You've been invited to a party hosted by someone very close to you—a best friend or a family member—someone you care about deeply. You arrive early to help, but when you walk in, you're surprised. The space isn't set up. The chairs are still stacked, and there's no festive atmosphere, and a few party preppers are at work. You approach someone you know who's helping organize the event, and ask, 'How can I support you? I want to help make sure everything's ready before the guests and the guest of honor arrive.'

"They reply, 'The chairs aren't set up yet. Can you take care of that?' You agree and begin setting up the chairs. You're halfway through when someone else approaches and says, 'Thank you for working on the chairs—it's looking great. But if you look around, you'll notice there are no decorations. I'd appreciate your help with that. Can you pause what you're doing and start decorating instead?'

"They add, 'At the end of the day, people can stand if needed. But without decorations, it won't feel like a party. We want it to feel special.' So, you stop setting up chairs and start hanging decorations.

"You're midway through, up on a ladder hanging lights, when a third person walks up and says, 'I need your help. Could you come down for a moment?' You hesitate, knowing the lights aren't finished, and they explain, 'I have the cake. It's huge, and if I carry it alone, I might drop it. I need another set of hands to get it safely in place.' So, you step away from the decorations, help carry the cake, and set it up. It looks perfect."

Once they've had a moment to consider the scenario, ask: "What's your reaction to that experience? What would you do next? And then after that?"

I've received a wide range of responses, each offering insight into how the candidate thinks, prioritizes, and manages competing demands.

One candidate said: "I didn't enjoy being interrupted, but I understood the logic. The chairs were important, the decorations added value, but the cake was critical. From a priority standpoint, it made sense to shift tasks. If it were up to me, I'd now work backward: finish the lights, then go back to the chairs. Even if not all the chairs get set up, guests could grab their own as needed." This response demonstrated adaptability and structured thinking.

Another candidate took a very different stance: "I was frustrated. I wanted to complete the task I was originally assigned. I was asked to set up chairs, and I didn't finish. Being pulled away felt disruptive. By the time someone asked me to help with the cake, I was honestly over it. I didn't help with the cake—I just kept working on the lights." This response revealed a strong desire for task completion, but also rigidity and resistance to shifting priorities.

The Party Scenario has proven to be an effective tool, not just for evaluating decision-making and time management but also for understanding how candidates respond to ambiguity, shifting expectations, and team dynamics under pressure. It opens up valuable conversations that go beyond rehearsed answers and into real insight. You can hear how differently people respond and learn a lot about how each will problem-solve, prioritize, and respond to challenges.

It goes without saying, scenarios are best when tailored to fit the role. The Party Scenario serves to surface the behavioral themes on which I will zero in during interviews.

There are no right answers. For highly structured roles demanding precision, you may be looking for someone who fits the profile of a person who wants to set up chairs from start to finish. In contrast, for a role that requires high levels of adaptability and multitasking, you might prefer a candidate who happily plans to rotate between various responsibilities. This is not a catch-all, however; if someone has a compelling explanation for their actions—even if it is not what you would typically expect for the role—it could offer valuable insight into how they might perform if they join the team.

Unpacking the Résumé

Reviewing a candidate's résumé and having them talk through their experience is essential. Pay close attention to alignment and consistency between what's written and what's shared. If you notice any discrepancies, make a point to address them directly and give the candidate an opportunity to clarify.

As mentioned earlier, a behavioral assessment, such as the **Predictive Index Behavioral Assessment,** informs the hiring profile and is incorporated into screening, interviewing, team dynamics, and coaching effectiveness. I've found it highly effective, particularly because it includes suggested interview questions tied to behavioral traits. I don't use all of them, but I typically select one to three that are relevant to the role. These help me either validate a behavioral strength or explore whether the candidate has the potential to grow in an area that may not come naturally to them. That's where I look for willingness, ability, and behavioral flexibility, whether the candidate has the capacity to act effectively in ways that may stretch beyond their default style.

Before you dive into the mechanics of structuring questions, pause for a moment and think back to the best conversations you've ever had—those that felt effortless, open, and honest. Those are the qualities you want in your interviews. You've already learned how to welcome candidates with compassion, frame challenges around real work, and coordinate thoughtfully across your team. Now it's time to give that warmth a clear path.

Structure doesn't mean stiffness. It's simply a way to honor both your time and the candidate's by focusing on what truly matters. When you group questions into a few central themes—each directly tied to the critical outcomes you need—you create a roadmap that keeps the dialogue both genuine and purposeful. Candidates feel guided, not grilled. You stay on point without losing the human spark that makes great talent shine.

So how do you translate that balance of empathy and rigor into an actionable plan? Let's explore one straightforward method for organizing your interview around themes—and see how it aligns seamlessly with your critical success factors.

Organizing the Interview

One method is to organize your session around themes. There are many valid methods, and using themes helps me remain consistent in what I'm evaluating across candidates. It provides for meaningful comparisons through a structured scoring framework. Additionally, the themes closely align with the critical success factors and key accountabilities listed in the job description.

Here's a sample list of **critical success factors** I've defined for a specific role at one of the most respected and successful Quick-Serve Restaurant organizations:

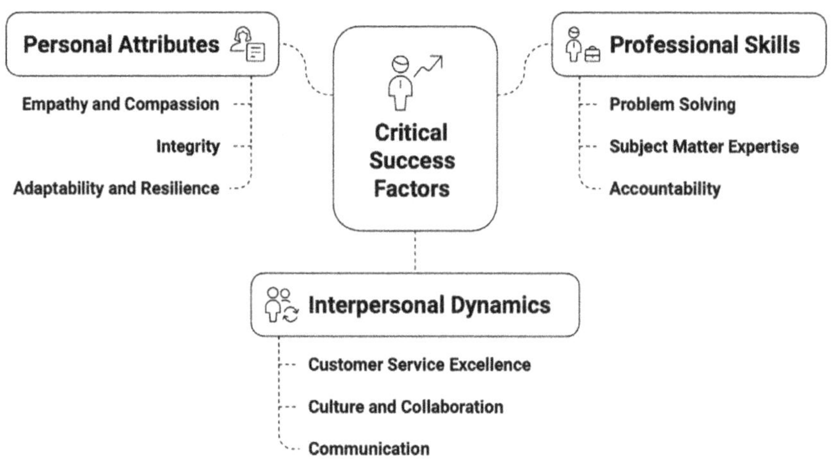

Note: Competencies shown are for example purposes only. Actual critical success factors may vary depending on your organization's context and priorities.

Keeping these themes handy helps me capture findings across candidates consistently. When it comes time to compare finalists—especially after several interviews—details can blur. This structured approach enables apple-to-apple comparison. If specific themes haven't been fully addressed, follow up with targeted questions to round out the assessment.

3.1 TAKE ACTION: Interviews are more than assessments—they're windows into how a candidate thinks, adapts, and aligns with your culture. List your version of critical success factors and tie those to specific tools discussed, so you are actively leveraging each to uncover and recognize a potential teammate. Use intentional icebreakers, real-world scenarios, and value-based questions to uncover more than rehearsed responses. Listen not just to what they say, but how they say it. Watch for patterns, red flags, and signs of growth potential. Being a fit on paper is simply not enough.

And before making an offer, ask yourself:

Will this person elevate our culture, own outcomes, and bring others along when it matters most? Will they thrive with me, with us, and grow where I envision placing them? Will they help us achieve our desired outcomes?"

CHAPTER 4

SETTING EXPECTATIONS

If your team keeps missing the mark, look at what you haven't said.

Remember those moments when your team felt unstoppable—deadlines met, ideas flowing, and energy high? It wasn't luck. It was the invisible contract you created by speaking clearly: defining success, clarifying roles, and setting the tone for how you work together. Yet too often, we lean on checklists and dashboards, assuming everyone will fill in the blanks. We leave expectations unstated and then wonder why progress stalls. What if the missing piece is simply the words we didn't say? Before we dive into milestones and metrics, let's pause to explore how the clarity of your voice shapes not just what your team does, but who they become.

If your team keeps missing the mark, look at what you haven't said.

As a leader, you shape more than output—you're shaping identity. You teach your team who to be through the culture you model and the clarity you provide.

Milestones set expectations, but it is more than that. Leaders commonly fall prey to technical errors, like giving **mixed messages** or no **preset expectations**. If something you say—or an action you take—differs materially from the culture you espouse, the communications you've made, or the milestones you've created, disengagement creeps in. More insidious is the leader who hesitates to clearly put expectations at stake for fear of missing the mark. They may even claim any outcome as their original intention, tragically damaging the culture you are building.

A small demonstration: You may have noticed there was no lead-in from the last chapter to this one. No setting of expectations. This may have been a big or small thing for you, however, there is an impact. Notice that impact on you. Think about that impact for your team. The E3 Effect values the setting of the expectations even more than the specific expectations themselves—if you don't, you risk missing the mark.

Become masterful at **setting expectations** that can work in any conversation. "Take care of each other" captures many situations and scenarios. Your team inhabits a workspace every day full of ups and downs, wins and losses. When they reflect, it's easy to measure against "did we take care of each other?"

The Stool: Creating a Strong Foundation

Back when I first heard Tony Robbins, he shared a concept about a stool that I now repurpose as a key indicator of team stability in my engagements. Realizing this random stool idea is still with me, informing my book on building world-class teams, is a full-circle moment.

Team stability is represented by the stool itself. Strength is given by the number of legs or how much weight the stool can bear. A two-legged stool topples over. One leg? Not even a stool.

One way to think about this—every win adds a leg. As a leader, your job is to create stability, continually increasing the number of legs under that principle, that metric, that vision; stabilizing the team.

Why is that important? Because challenges are on their way: companies shift direction, teams pivot, legs get knocked out. We've all experienced the loss of dissolving responsibilities. If you have enough legs, you'll still be stable.

The E3 practice of tying North Star principles to leg-producing wins generates multi-legged stability. Further, our leadership development tools provide the shortest path to the flywheel effect, supporting world-class teams that sustain over time.

Creating Clarity

Inherent in organizations are forces that we as leaders can and cannot control. That is a given, but what is not given is the ability to leverage the intersection into insights that inform our next actions. At any given moment, we have the opportunity to create clarity out of confusion, uncertainty, or even a typical workday. This tactic provides a precise place to stand when other realities are at play in framing the message your team will carry forward to your collective goal.

Using the clarity quadrant as a framework that helps leaders create clarity, taking three things into consideration, both in and out of your control, from positive to negative:

1. Y-Axis is an Evolution Continuum (Operations, Deadlines, Metrics)
2. X-Axis is a Time Continuum (Accelerate, Drag, Maximize, Optimize)
3. Drive towards the North Star on the positive continuum for both

At any moment in time, you can assess the current state, then choose how to move the team from there toward the North Star. This means knowing how to pivot—how to switch gears—to ensure your team can meet changing expectations.

Perhaps the plan was to roll out a new feature or launch a functionality that would enable an efficient workflow and enhance customer experience. However, the product team missed the deadline.

Then what? The business still expects the customer experience to improve. Some of that is within your control. Some of it's not. Given this reality, how do you guide your team with clarity to a place closer to your North Star?

Honesty plays a big part, as does humility, especially regarding what's in your control and your messaging to the team.

IN PRACTICE: Something like, "Hey, you know that product thing we were waiting on to make this easier? It's delayed. But we still need to move in that direction. So we're going to figure out how to do that, starting now.

"We're going to create some attainable metrics that you all will help design. Then, we'll start moving in the direction we need to go. When the product solution arrives, it won't just make things easier—it will amplify what we already understand and do well."

We're making a meaningful difference for our customers. And there's a tone to how we communicate that. There's intentionality when it comes to delivering this kind of feedback and redirecting a team.

As a leader, you create those expectations—or the company sets them—and you have to execute. So ask yourself: How much leeway can you give the team?

I've explained it this way: "We have this much space to work in. We can turn left or right. We can go fast. We can slow down to think, plan, and strategize. But we can't just stop; the business keeps moving. And we can't go all out if the pace of the business isn't there to support it."

On the left and right, the business defines who we are and what we do. That's our lane. It has structure. It has limits. When you teach team members to think this way, they become more open to the "why" behind a shift, a pivot, or a redirection. They get the context.

That's why it's critical as a leader to be open, to be accountable, to set clear, proactive expectations, and to live up to your part of the bargain. But it's just as critical that you hold your team accountable, too.

Managing Up

It is imperative to develop teams to become comfortable with managing up. Remember the individual who cried earlier in the story, and we used the 1-to-10 Net Promoter Score (NPS) system? Before we developed the 1-to-10 scale, we reviewed our behavioral profiles. And with that, we discussed—openly, objectively—how to manage up.

So I taught her how to manage me, what I need from her to be able to help her at the highest level possible. It creates **vulnerability**, which builds relatedness, trust, and connection.

IN PRACTICE: If I observe a notable lesson with one of my team members, I may explore the value in sharing with a larger group. I check in with the team member, outlining the value and requesting permission to share. They know they can say no, yes, or counteroffer anonymously, or "Please sanitize it." It's powerful to have someone say, "That's fine. I'd love for you to share this so no one else experiences what I did." And I honor that. How you do that demonstrates culture. It is your day-to-day responsibility to support the relationship success factor.

4.1 TAKE ACTION: Develop a **30-60-90-day plan** with your leadership team to define, socialize, and activate expectations that align with your cultural principles and business outcomes. Include:

- A shared vocabulary around what "**excellence**" looks like.
- Scenarios that test how your team adjusts when expectations shift.
- Coaching rhythms that reinforce identity and accountability.

Be sure your plan includes measurable outcomes—because without them, you're communicating values, not operational clarity.

To close this chapter, opportunity exists: next time your team misses the mark, make a list of five things you realize went unsaid, then find a way to share them with your team.

Enable Self-Assessment

Before we move into the next phase, I want to provide you with a structure to pause and reflect. This self-assessment is designed to help you take an honest look at how you're showing up in the **Enable** phase. Scoring high across the board isn't the expectation—the goal is clarity. The more clearly you understand your strengths and areas for growth, the more intentionally you can lead.

This is your chance to invest in yourself, because the better you know where you stand, the better equipped you'll be to elevate those around you.

Scoring Scale:

1. **Highly Capable** (I consistently excel in this area)
2. **Strong** (I perform well, but see room for improvement)
3. **Developing** (I have some experience but need more growth)
4. **Needs Improvement** (I struggle in this area and need focused effort)
5. **Significant Opportunity for Growth** (I need to learn and develop in this area)

Instructions:

- For each statement, assign a score from 1 to 5 based on the scale above.
- Total your scores for each section.
- Reflect on your overall performance and identify areas for improvement.

1. Culture & Leadership

- **I actively foster a culture where team members feel valued, supported, and engaged.**

  Score: ____

- **I recognize signs of disengagement and take proactive steps to address them.**

  Score: ____

- **I create an environment that fosters innovation, encourages feedback, and promotes continuous improvement.**

  Score: ____

- **I lead with emotional intelligence, ensuring that my team members feel heard and understood.**

  Score: ____

- **I set clear expectations and acknowledge contributions in a way that inspires performance.**

  Score: ____

  Total Score for Culture & Leadership: ____ / 25

2. Defining Success & Driving Performance

- **I establish measurable goals and clear expectations for my team.**

  Score: ____

- **I help my team understand how their work aligns with the organization's broader objectives.**

  Score: ____

- **I provide consistent, structured feedback that supports growth and accountability.**

  Score: ____

- **I ensure that my team experiences small wins that build momentum toward larger achievements.**

  Score: ____

- **I hold myself and others accountable while fostering a culture of trust and integrity.**

  Score: ____

  Total Score for Defining Success & Driving Performance: ____ / 25

3. Building & Scaling Teams

- **I hire and develop talent that aligns with both our culture and strategic objectives.**

  Score: ____

- **I conduct interviews that assess problem-solving abilities, adaptability, and alignment with our values.**

  Score: ____

- **I utilize assessments and behavioral insights to inform hiring and leadership decisions.**

  Score: ____

- **I focus on developing leaders within my team to ensure long-term organizational success.**

  Score: ____

- **I create a work environment where team members feel empowered to take ownership and make decisions.**

  Score: ____

  Total Score for Building & Scaling Teams: ____ / 25

4. Empowerment & Ownership

- **I empower my team to take full ownership of projects, decisions, and outcomes.**

  Score: ____

- **I provide the right balance of autonomy and structured support to my team.**

  Score: ____

- **I encourage individuals to document, refine, and improve workflows for greater efficiency.**

  Score: ____

- **I offer coaching and development opportunities that support both professional and personal growth.**

  Score: ____

- **I celebrate wins and ensure that team members feel their contributions are recognized.**

  Score: ____

  Total Score for Empowerment & Ownership: ____ / 25

  Overall "Enable" Score for Phase 1: ____ / 100

Reflection and Next Steps

1. Review Your Scores:

- **80–100:** Significant growth opportunities exist. Consider seeking mentorship, training, or leadership
- **60–79:** Key areas need attention. Identify one or two specific actions to take in the next thirty days.
- **40–59:** You are performing well but have opportunities to deepen your leadership and team development.

- **Below 40:** You have a strong foundation in enabling high performance. Continue refining and scaling your impact.

2. Identify Your Focus Area:

- What is one immediate action you will take to strengthen your leadership?

  ____

  ____

  ____

- What is one long-term goal you aim to achieve based on your results?

  ____

  ____

  ____

3. Continue Your Leadership Journey:

If you're seeking additional insights and strategies to accelerate your growth as a leader, my team and I at PangeaEffect offer resources to support your journey. This is an open invitation to explore what's possible for you and your team.

4. Stay Committed to Growth:

Leadership is a continuous journey. Every step forward, big or small, contributes to your development. Keep learning, stay curious, and continue enabling those around you to achieve greatness.

You are the breakthrough waiting to happen. Go make it real.

PHASE 2: EMPOWER

Building Mechanisms of Trust

CHAPTER 5

CHANGE MINDSET

Change isn't the problem; your team's resistance is.

You've rolled out new tools, restructured teams, and rallied around bold initiatives—only to watch resistance creep in like an unwanted guest. You tracked every milestone, crafted every message, yet something still stalled. It isn't a flaw in your strategy; it's a human response to the uncertainty and disruption that change brings.

Before we unpack the stages of that resistance, pause for a moment and consider what lies beneath your project plans: the stories your team tells itself about stability, the habits they cling to for comfort, and the subtle fear of losing what once felt secure. These are the currents that shape how real people respond when familiar routines shift.

In this chapter, we'll turn our attention to that human side of change—acknowledging denial, anger, bargaining, depression, and finally acceptance. By leaning into the very emotions most leaders try to bypass, you'll discover how to transform resistance into momentum, using clarity, compassion, and a gardener's patience to guide your people through the journey ahead.

There are many types of change, and one of the leadership nutrients you will manage is your team's personal and collective relationship to and response around change in an organization.

Borrowing from proven methods not usually applied to the business world can provide leverage for such a process. In the area of change management, an approach I've come to rely on is one many people are sadly familiar with—the **Kübler-Ross grief cycle**, also known as the **five stages of grief**.

Kübler-Ross' Five Stages of Grief

1. Denial
2. Anger
3. Bargaining
4. Depression
5. Acceptance

It may seem odd to look at the **five stages of grief** for change management, yet disruption in the workplace can evoke many responses and feelings that mirror, on a micro level, loss of the way things have been. This may be a loss of comfort, routine, or control. Being clear that workplace change does not equate to personal loss, we nevertheless assert that experiencing these stages as they relate to professional and group dynamics may prepare individuals for organizational change, now or in the future. There is often an element of **denial**. Not everyone experiences this—some are very comfortable with change and jump right in.

Anticipate and prepare for those who try to avoid it. They may be triggered, experience confusion, or even feel fear or shock in response to the change. From there, they may move into **anger**, where frustration, irritation, and anxiety begin to surface. Even when present, there are actions to take and an invitation for them to identify and diffuse these emotions.

Next is the **bargaining phase**. Some team members may come back to you and ask, "Is there something we can do to change this a bit?" They might tell their own story about why the change won't work for them, or try to influence others to deny or push back against the change. At the core of this, what leaders need to understand is that people are struggling to find meaning. They want to know that they can handle the change, that they can fit in, that they still have a place. These are essential components to recognize as you tend your garden.

The next stage is **depression**. At this point, they might feel overwhelmed. They might experience hostility toward the change, a sense of helplessness, or try to move to a different group or team to avoid being impacted. However, after navigating the changes that the disturbance represents, teams have the opportunity to reach the final stage: **acceptance**.

As a leader, your role is to support your team members, department, and organization in navigating these five stages, allowing individuals the space to experience them. These responses are natural; they're human. If you don't allow people to be human, you'll struggle to get the buy-in you need for them to meet the critical success factors you set earlier. Acceptance is the goal. Change has a way of revealing the weak points on your team; I am grateful for the clarity this brings on where to focus my attention. Once the team has arrived at acceptance, you can begin to explore new options together.

Creating Hope During Times of Change

Leading Through Change

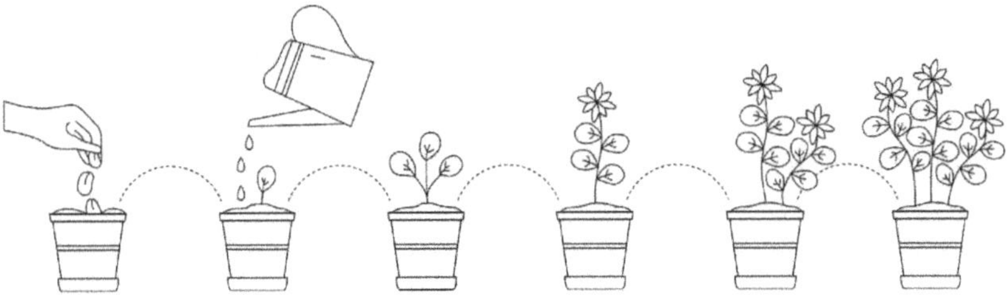

Resistance
Team resists change and feels uncertain

Define Change
Clearly communicate the change and its impact

Enlist Influencers
Gain support from key team members

Communicate Hope
Share a positive vision for the future

Provide Clarity
Offer a clear timeline and expectations

Acceptance
Team embraces change and feels optimistic

You've guided your team through denial, anger, bargaining, and even the weight of depression—and you've seen firsthand how each stage can stall momentum or spark breakthroughs. Now comes the most vital act of leadership: planting seeds of optimism that will carry everyone forward.

Before we talk tools and timelines, pause to consider what hope looks like in your organization. It isn't a hollow promise or empty pep talk. True hope springs from clarity, the belief that each person's contribution matters, and collaboration. In this section, you'll learn how to define the change in terms your team can embrace, enlist the voices that drive culture, and create the conditions for genuine optimism—so that acceptance doesn't just end the cycle of grief, but marks the start of something better.

With a new plan in place, there needs to be hope that this new approach, this change, will work and be successful. From there, the team and individuals can begin to normalize into the new experience or phase, where the change is fully integrated.

There are a few things to consider as you begin thinking about this. First, **define the change**. How big is it? How much of a disruption is it to your everyday operation or to an individual's daily work life? As a leader, the change may not feel like a big deal to you because you're the one implementing it. However, even leaders sometimes struggle to accept change and may experience their own version of the five stages of grief.

We need to allow space for that, too. You must be mindful of how you're communicating. It's okay to show vulnerability and acknowledge that you're also figuring it out, but **your message must always contain hope**. As a leader, I encourage you to look at change from the team's perspective. Look at it from the individual's perspective—not your own. You may have some aha moments or insights that can help your team members and department navigate the change.

Another critical component is knowing who your **key influencers** are. There's usually someone the group naturally gravitates toward to interpret the impact and how to process it. You want to identify your key influencers, and sometimes it makes sense to get them on board before announcing the change to the whole team. You can do this by introducing the idea: "Here's what we're doing, here's what we're thinking." Leave space to co-design the change with them. Be mindful of who these influencers are, and get their support early on.

If you can't get them on board, you'll need to neutralize their influence. How can you keep them neutral toward the change? Train them to understand that if someone comes to them with concerns, their role is to redirect that person to you or to another designated leader who can help navigate the change. These are helpful strategies whenever a meaningful change is occurring within the team.

Next, write down what the change will be. Use whatever tool works best for you: PowerPoint, video, whiteboard—anything that helps communicate the change effectively. An impactful visual of the current state versus the future state can be very helpful. Review the plan with the team. This provides them with the necessary information to process the change. As they move through the five stages of grief, they'll be able to revisit the material, digest it, and come back with questions.

The next part of the change mindset is preparing for instantaneous change. One moment, we're heading in one direction, and the next, we pivot. Sometimes it's gradual, but there's usually a clear turning point when the change starts to take effect, and the impact begins. It's crucial that you, as a leader, provide clarity on the expected timeframe for adopting and integrating the change into behaviors, language, actions, and supporting tools or materials. Remember, people need time to process their emotions. Some are fast processors: they get it in a few minutes, and they're good to go. But most people need more time. So, you need to know your team, and they need to experience that you know them.

As we established in an earlier chapter, building trust is key. Knowing your team members is part of that culture. In this case, understanding the amount of time they need to adjust and providing it is important. Of course, sometimes that's not possible when an initiative comes to a halt, or a significant course change needs to happen with little to no notice.

CONVERSATION PLAYBOOK:

When it's appropriate to be transparent with your team: "I would have given you more notice if I could, but I just found out myself. I want to make sure you're informed as soon as possible, and we'll work together to adopt this upcoming change. Let me tell you about the change. And by the way, here's the document that will be referenced. Now that we have this, it will take some time to process, and I will break it down into manageable steps—by role—to ensure you can absorb the changes in your day-to-day work, from logging in each day to your specific tasks. I'll also clarify what's not going to change."

The point of highlighting what stays consistent adds a leg to the stool when others will be removed with the change. Communicating in this way provides a foundation and a sense of stability. No matter how small that is, it matters.

Say: "Hey, we're still going to be logging into the same system. Your usernames and passwords will remain the same. When you log in, you'll still see the same tools or screens. There may be some changes in the wording on the screens, and some fields may be rearranged for display purposes. We're changing the workflow, but the actual output we're aiming for remains the same. The goal is to drive efficiency. I'd love to have your partnership in giving feedback to the product team,"—if we're talking about a system update, for example—"your input is valuable."

Managing Expectations

This brings us back to setting expectations and involving people in the improvement process. Whether someone chooses to step up or not is ultimately their decision, but by offering the opportunity, they're given the chance to feel heard and to contribute. That's why it's so important to set clear expectations around what changes you want from the team, and also what the team can expect from leadership.

As much as we want the team to understand what they need to know about the change and how it will impact them, they also need to understand how leadership will support them through that change.

Ultimately, it all starts with culture. If you have a thriving culture—where change is accepted as inevitable and seen as part of the process— you're setting yourself up for growth. A business that's changing has the opportunity to grow. A company that's staying the same is at risk of stagnating and falling behind the competition. The question then becomes: How do you create a culture where change is inevitable, yet people are set up for success? How do you want your team to perceive and receive the change?

Bruce Tuckman's Leadership Model

I was first introduced to a leadership model by my son's work staffing National Youth Leadership Training (NYLT) through the Scouting program. Developed by psychologist **Bruce Tuckman,** I found it to be particularly useful as a leadership model detailing the stages of team development. You might be familiar with it.

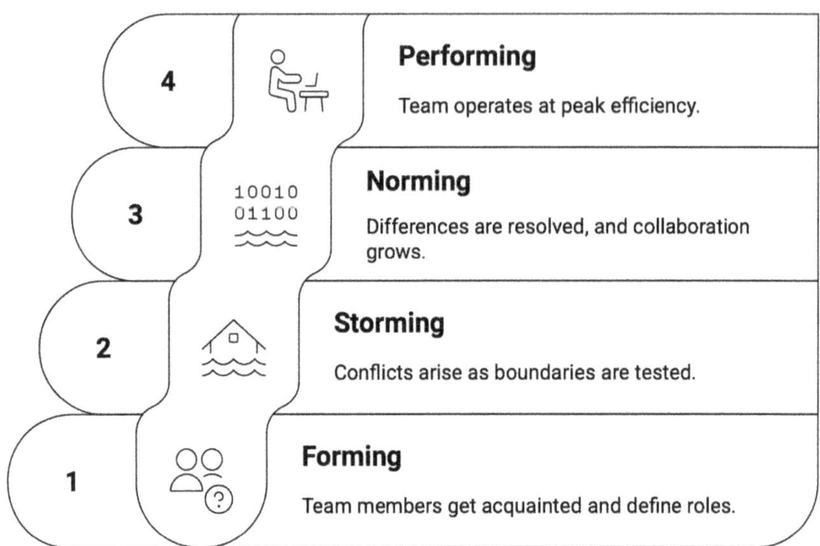

Source: Bruce Tuckman's Leadership Model, stages 1–4.

There are five stages in total before reaching a stable, ongoing workflow: **Forming, Storming, Norming, Performing, and Adjourning.**

- **Forming** is the stage when team members are getting acquainted and defining their roles. Depending on the nature of the change, they may need to return to this phase even if they've been with the organization for years. If their role is shifting, or the people or tools they work with are changing, they're back in Forming mode.

- **Storming** comes next. This phase is when conflicts arise as people test boundaries and adjust to the new situation. This overlaps with the five stages of grief that we discussed earlier.

- After storming comes **Norming**, where differences begin to be resolved, and collaboration starts to grow. At this stage, you'll begin to feel the team aligning. Resistance decreases, and you begin to see the benefits of shared understanding and cooperation.

- And then there's **Performing**. Once you get past the earlier stages, this is when the team operates at peak efficiency. Have you ever had a team where they've reached a point where you no longer have to tell them precisely what to do?

- The last stage is **Adjourning**. Some teams form for a limited time. It might be a task force created for a special project or a temporary team explicitly assembled to lead a change effort. At some point, that team will disband. That marks the end of the team. Some people experience this as a kind of mourning.

The thing about these stages is that, as leaders, your role is to help your teams navigate through **Forming**, **Storming**, **Norming**, and **Performing**. At any given time, parts of the team might be in different stages, especially in larger teams.

This process isn't always linear. A team in the performing stage can revert to the Storming or Forming stage if significant changes occur. Imagine there's a new process, new members, or shifting priorities. Resistance or disagreements might arise, pushing the team back into the Storming stage. Then, as those issues are worked through, they return to Norming, where collaboration grows again, and then move back to performing. It's helpful to know that teams cycle through these stages.

Leading With Emotional Intelligence

As a leader, one of your responsibilities is to instill confidence in your team. And that starts by having confidence in yourself. When you communicate with confidence, hope, and empathy (when you bring **emotional intelligence** into the conversation), you avoid being **tone-deaf** and instead show your team that you're in tune with how they're feeling.

From Tone-Deaf to Emotionally Intelligent Leader

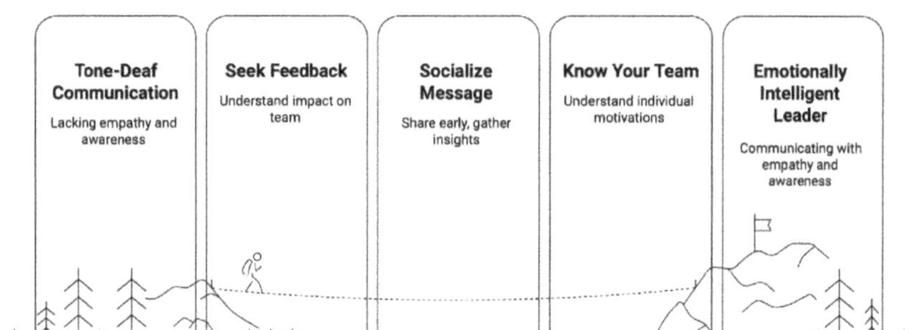

Many years ago, I was a younger leader, and I had to communicate a change to the team. Honestly, it didn't go very well. I don't even remember exactly what the change was now, but it was significant for the team. One of the managers on my team—someone with a very high level of empathy—came to me afterward. She said, "Daniel, what you just communicated to the team came across as tone-deaf."

I didn't understand what she meant, so I stayed curious. Let's call this manager, "Jean." I said, "Jean, tell me more. I want to understand what you mean by 'tone-deaf.' I've never heard that feedback before."

She explained that while I had clearly articulated what the change was and what the new expectations would be, something important was missing: There was no listening, no awareness of how the team was receiving the message, and no shift in my communication to be with the team in the moment, rather than just lecturing or delivering information *at* them.

What I took away from that experience was the importance of **socializing** the message, starting with one or a few key people, to the greatest extent possible. Of course, some things are too confidential to share early, but when you *can* share, at *any* level, it's important to socialize the message.

Second, know your team. Get to know the people—what makes them tick, what's important to them. Which part of the job do they love most? Which part do they value the most? If I were going to impact that part, I would make sure to acknowledge it directly.

IN PRACTICE: I might say something like: "Hey, I know this is a part of your role that you enjoy and excel at, and we're over-performing in this area (if that's the case). Still, because of a strategic initiative at the organizational level…" Notice how I tie it back to something bigger: "You are a critical player in this change, and here's what you need to know about your role and how it will impact your day-to-day."

With that kind of framing, people can begin to see themselves in the change. If they don't, there may still be many natural follow-up conversations, but the key idea is: Don't be tone-deaf. Know your team. Know what's important to them. Know which parts of the job are most fulfilling and which parts are least fulfilling or most challenging. Perhaps the change will *eliminate* some of the least fulfilling or most challenging aspects of the job. Perhaps it enables them to lean more into their strengths and spend more time working within their zone of excellence.

That's a positive message. "This change is going to happen, and yes, it will impact us—but here's what you need to know: Our strengths are in areas like quality, speed, or efficiency (whatever those metrics are), and this change will allow us to focus more on those strengths and spend more time doing what we do best. So, let me tell you about the change..." That would be an effective way to begin.

5.1 TAKE ACTION: Change Mindset

1. **Map the Emotional Journey.** Think about a current or upcoming change your team is facing. Identify where each team member might be within the Kübler-Ross grief cycle. Use this as a guide to tailor your support and communication accordingly.

2. **Socialize the Message Early.** Identify one or two key influencers on your team. Share the change with them first, gather feedback, and

invite them into the co-design process. Their early alignment will help shape broader team buy-in.

3. **Communicate with Empathy and Clarity.** Draft a message that acknowledges the disruption the change may bring while reinforcing what will remain the same. Ground the message in hope, and be clear about the next steps.

4. **Define the Change Visually.** Create a simple side-by-side visual of the current state vs. the future state. This could be a slide, whiteboard drawing, or short video—whatever fits your team best. Use it to anchor conversations and reduce ambiguity.

5. **Set Expectations and Offer Support.** Clarify both what's expected from your team during the transition and what they can expect from you. Let them know how and when they can raise questions or concerns—and follow through with real-time support.

Change is often outside of your control, however, within your control lies your navigation and the impact of your team's resistance. These strategies can help.

CHAPTER 6

ACCESS TO KNOWLEDGE AND RESOURCES

If your team can't think for itself, you're doing it for them.

You've set clear expectations, guided your people through change, and planted the seeds of hope, but even the most motivated team can stall if they don't know where to find the answers. Think back to the last time someone on your team asked, "Where do I find that document?" or "How am I supposed to do this?" In those moments, you don't just lose time; you risk eroding the confidence and momentum you've worked so hard to build.

In this chapter, we'll tackle the often-overlooked backbone of high performance: providing your team with instant access to the knowledge and resources they need to think and act independently. When you remove friction—when every tool, workflow, and best practice sits at your people's fingertips—you transform dependency into autonomy, confusion into clarity, and hesitation into decisive action.

Knowledge of how to do the work is essential. Teams require tools and resources, which must be readily accessible.

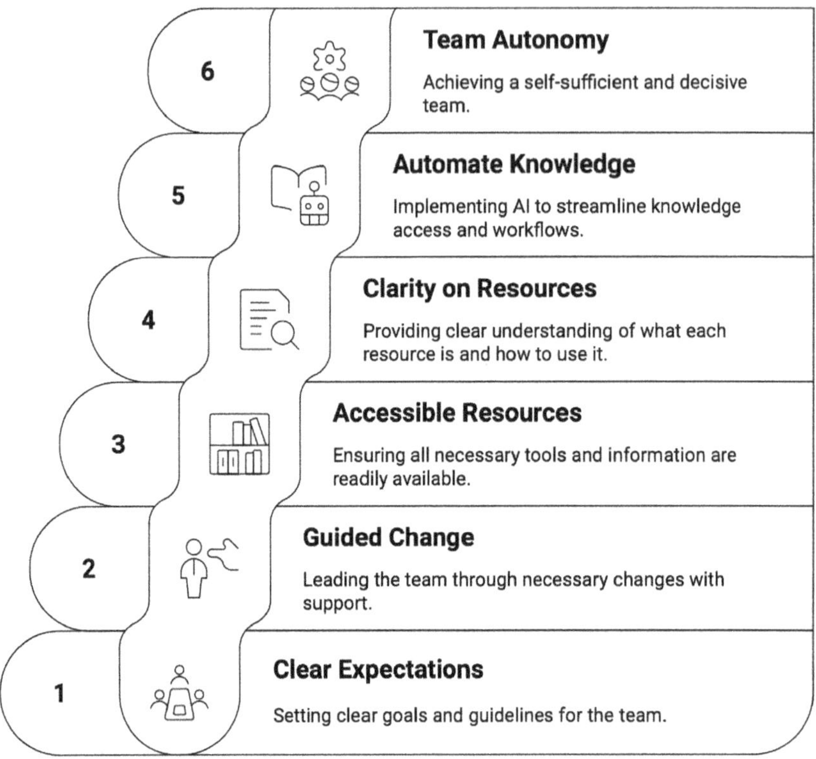

Team members must be aware of these tools and resources. The more granular the task, the more critical it is to have easily accessible information. Greater complexity increases the need for simple, reliable sources of guidance. The more infrequent or rare the task, the more the team will rely on accessible, clearly organized information.

In today's environment, where artificial intelligence (AI) is emerging as a tool to predict workflows, guide next steps, and support task execution, there's an increasing opportunity to automate these knowledge systems. That's something for organizations to go after if they have the resources. (If they don't, PangeaEffect has resources to support you.)

Specificity Is Key

Early in my career, I would say, "Let me know if you need anything" or "Here's a folder with all the information." Have you ever done that? Just dropped everything in one place and said, "Take a look when you can"?

What I've learned is that this direction is vague, disempowering, and overwhelming. Team members may not feel they have the time to thoroughly review and make sense of it. Ask yourself: Is the information organized in a way that is memorable and easy to use? Can someone look at it for five seconds and know exactly what to do next?

We want to avoid vague directions. Instead, here's how to think about knowledge and resources: I assert that teams and the business benefit when every individual has **one hundred percent clarity** on:

- What the resource is
- Where it can be found
- How to access it
- What it means when they do
- Who it's for: internal/external

How do we get from here to there? We have all experienced the trial-by-fire hiring process of sitting with colleagues watching a range of different experiences. At some point, you're told, "Okay, now do it yourself." Side-by-side observation can be disruptive; it slows output and is inconsistent.

Creating a **single source of truth** is necessary and foundational to a high-performing team. At one organization that lacked such a tool, I began by asking the team to identify specifically which items should be included in a resource they could rely upon—things like processes, workflows, methodologies, and general knowledge. This would help answer frequently asked questions, handle more complex issues, and define escalation rules, among other things. Essentially, it would become the **knowledge base**. We will do a deep dive into that process in Chapter 7.

Balancing Empowerment and Risk

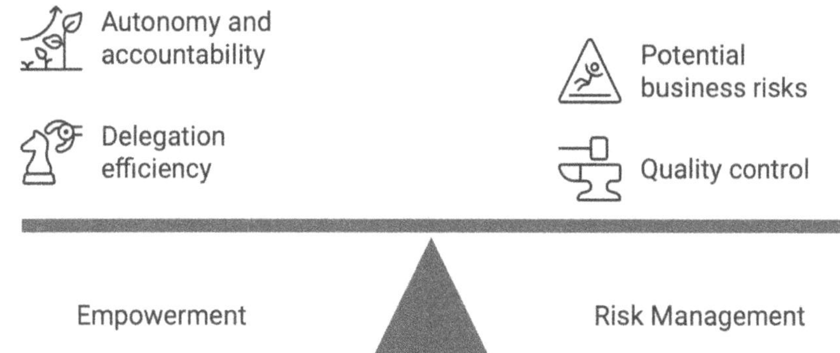

You've worked to give your team instant access to the right information—curation tools, building a single source of truth, and mapping out the critical, frequent, or complex workflows. Yet you may have noticed a new challenge emerge: some people hang back, unsure if they're allowed to act, while others dive in and occasionally overstep. In those moments, the issue isn't a lack of resources—it's finding the sweet spot between trust and caution.

Before we dive into strategies and examples, take a moment to consider how you decide what to share, with whom, and when. The real art of leadership lies not just in handing over knowledge, but in calibrating the boundaries that let your team move quickly without putting the organization at risk. In the pages ahead, you'll learn how to empower smartly—so autonomy and accountability grow together, not at odds.

Teams must have access to what they need. The only exception is when the information is not appropriate for them to know: if it's highly confidential, pertains to another department, or might derail or confuse them. You should be aiming for **clear expectations**, knowledge that's relevant to the person, delivered at the right time, in the right way. A good leader uses both emotional intelligence and wisdom to determine what knowledge and resources to share.

This does, however, raise the question: Where is the line between a team member's ability to make decisions and take action when they're empowered and when there's too much risk for the business for them to have that level of empowerment? And that is the line right there. It requires a **risk analysis**.

Instead of talking about knowledge, I'm going to talk about **delegation** for a minute. A few decades ago, I was a horrible delegator. I thought everything had to be done to the nth degree, that no one could do it like I could do it, and that no one would do it as well as I would do it. Very quickly, I became too busy and was unable to attend to the most critical tasks because I was overwhelmed with all the small and mid-sized tasks.

Luckily, for me, another leader saw my struggle and took the time to pour development into me. I am grateful to this mentor and the massive difference delegation has made in my career, in my bandwidth, and in my ability to lead and have time to build culture, and have time to connect.

The lesson from this is: If something can be done eighty percent as well as I do it, and that would be good enough, then go ahead and *delegate* it to someone who will do it at eighty percent of your capacity. You can review it until you align and calibrate on the deliverables. You can even develop them if they're at seventy percent and you need to push them a bit, but next time they'll hit it. However, if the work requires one hundred percent, I keep it to myself or have them take it to eighty percent and take it across the line myself.

This principle applies to **empowerment.** What level of risk comes with the empowerment you're giving them? If there's a fail point that occurs, they overstep their empowerment or provide it to the wrong person, or a mistake is made, what risk does that bring to the business and team? What about your reputation, theirs, your leaders? Those would be the questions I would ask myself.

Let me give you an example. I had the opportunity to work at The Ritz-Carlton. It was one of the great privileges of my life to be steeped in that culture. Ritz-Carlton is renowned for its system of knowledge-sharing and empowerment. One of the ways they do this is by providing team members with explicit permission—and the tools—to take thoughtful action on behalf of the guest.

At the Ritz-Carlton, every team member had a daily allowance they could use to go the extra mile for a guest. For example, every guest-facing or back-of-house team member had up to $2,000 to spend on creating an exceptional experience. That could mean providing a dessert when you learn it's a guest's birthday, or even running to the store because you discovered a guest's favorite cereal is Froot Loops. The guest finds it in the room with milk in the mini fridge, a bowl on the table with a handwritten note: *"We want to make sure it feels like home while you're here."* That's an empowered employee taking initiative.

Some changes can be communicated in advance. Others are so sensitive that there is too much risk of the message getting out, which is why it's communicated immediately afterward. You bring in your leaders immediately before the change, and you communicate the change to them first. Then, after that, they are part of communicating with the team. So that would be just an example of responding to risk assessment. We'll discuss discernment further in the next chapter.

So, what does this strategy look like for your company? It could involve decision-making authority, empowering your team so they don't have to rely on someone else to move forward. Can you clear a roadblock? Can you flatten a speed bump that's preventing them from completing their work? In other words, wherever there's friction (delays, redundant work, or red tape), is there an action you, as a leader, can take to empower that team member with knowledge and resources? Can you trust that they'll use that power appropriately?

Think back to Chapter 4, where we talked about defining success, critical success factors, and milestones. Are you empowering your team enough to navigate those challenges successfully? Do they need more knowledge? More resources?

6.1 TAKE ACTION: To have your team think for themselves, make it a habit to ask them, "What's missing that would make a difference for you?" Train them to get with people in other roles with different perspectives, and report back. You'll hear insights that give you a more complete picture, where additional knowledge or resources could be applied to further empower and enable the team.

CHAPTER 7

DISCERNMENT

Discernment is not just a skill; it's a force multiplier.

Discernment touches every aspect of leadership, especially for leaders out to build the high-performing teams we discuss here. The ability to use discernment individually and collectively takes every outcome and multiplies its impact. Just as your leader relies on you to apply discernment to reduce friction, you rely on your team for the same. The type of development that hones this skill provides regular watering to your garden and reduces unforced errors. Let's take it for a spin.

At Disney, there's a car-driving amusement ride, Autopia. Each driver works the steering, brakes, and accelerator. The goal is amusement, so how do they reduce friction? How do they minimize crashes? A center rail guides riders along the track, no matter their age or experience. This setup mirrors a **discernment training system,** allowing autonomy while minimizing risk.

The rail keeps you on track, allowing you to steer side-to-side, within parameters. The brake and accelerator allow the driver to modulate how abruptly or smoothly changes in speed are made.

Work-world discernment training lies in building a thoughtful consideration of actions that have impacts. On the ride, if you don't modulate your speed properly, you're going to get hit. Your discernment is in direct proportion to how hard.

Mastery lies in adapting to the prescribed limits and becoming comfortable to the point of unconscious competence. The discernment level attained can be observed by light guidance, resulting in smooth sailing with minimal friction. Willful disregard of the rail and unconsidered modulation is an entirely different issue for a leader to address (covered in Chapters 1 and 2) when defining culture and success.

Your light guidance lives in your check-ins. As a leader, you provide the centering rail for your team. The person you hire drives their car as part of their role, working within the parameters that you set up. The organization has parameters that you are managing at the same time, just as you position your garden in the sunlight. High discernment empowers your team to function optimally.

We rely heavily on discernment in life. The question is: Are you using discernment at work, and are you applying it intentionally, purposefully, and thoughtfully?

Discernment in Upper-Level Leadership

Some decisions may be made higher in the organization and by another set of leaders, then funneled to you, and then from you to the frontline team members. It is, therefore, critical to hire people with natural discernment and continue to develop it directly.

The higher the level, the more discernment required. Part of your skill here is assessing the discernment level of others. In the Party Scenario, be clear about what solutions and reasoning highlight this skill. Look for elements that facilitate smooth processing and seamless experiences that translate into working within your organization and that you could imagine working well with all levels.

Discernment in Practice

Little happens in isolation; this example shows how I wove this skill into developing a team as a whole. Thinking about these elements in concert keeps you generating real work scenarios. I joined a team of five, including four frontline team members. It was an established organization growing at a blistering pace. The plan was to grow the team and then "10x" the business over the next four years. First, I assessed the existing skills, tools, resources, and institutional knowledge, starting with **side-by-sides** with each team member.

I learned that each worked differently. There was no **consistent methodology** for completing tasks. Best practices were inconsistently applied and individualized. Sparse documentation had multiple versions, and they had never considered a **single source of truth**. This is one of my favorite problems as it is foundational and required to grow or scale. The solution is a secret passageway to developing world-class high-performing teams.

> A **single source of truth** is one definitive place where the most accurate and up-to-date version of information lives. It eliminates confusion caused by multiple versions stored across personal folders or drives. Whether it's a CRM tool, knowledge article, digital employee handbook, or Standard Operating Procedure (SOP), a single Source of Truth ensures everyone is aligned, reducing errors and enabling growth at scale.

Another sure sign of a team ripe for development is reliance on veterans to casually side-by-side each new hire until they are told, "Okay, now go do it yourself." At some point, the training of new hires must be reckoned with. This intersection is where we pick up our discernment thread.

Once you cement the buy-in to the concept of a **single source of truth**, activate discernment training with all participants identifying which items should be included in that source—things like processes, workflows, methodologies, and general knowledge. This captures frequently asked questions, helps handle more complex issues, and defines escalation rules. Eventually, it becomes the **knowledge base**.

IN PRACTICE: Create a shared document (a Google Sheet) to organize efforts. Columns in our sheet included:

Google Sheet Columns
A. The name of the article/topic B. Brief description/objective C. Submitted by D. Drafted Y/N E. Revised Y/N F. Approved Y/N G. Published to

This provided us with a clear **roadmap** for moving forward:

Milestone One– Build the List

Set a time and, in the spaces between the work, add topics that you would have needed when you first started. In three weeks, the team identified eighty topics.

Milestone Two– Drafting Articles

Get consensus on clear descriptions for column two and set up a system for ownership and cadence that supports the daily activities ongoingly. This team gave priority to the submitter and from there, set a goal to each draft one article weekly.

Milestone Three– Approvals and Publishing

Completed articles populate the Single Source of Truth. Share editing rights, but designate final approval to a trusted (discerning) role. Share the resources across the organization for greater sun positioning.

Milestone Four– Support the Process

The key here is the building **process**; it creates a **flywheel effect**: The more teams engage in this work, the more motivated they become to build, especially when they personally contribute to the quality of life at work. The point is: building the winning mentality.

Milestone Five– Leveraging the Knowledge Base

Teams first discern the knowledge base as a single source of truth, then second, what kind of content belongs in it. As a result, ownership blooms, aligned with its purpose and content.

The forming and norming of the first few milestones become performing as articles are kept as operationally current as possible, despite not having full-time resources to dedicate.

The true power of this tool is seen when the next new hire can navigate and self-pace the majority of the foundationals by leveraging the content that is no longer tribal, but a thing to be relied upon.

Trainees can even be empowered to look for inconsistencies and outdated information–**scavenger hunt** style: How many issues can you find? Can you categorize them differently? Incorporate both interactive learning and continuous improvement right from the start.

This was discernment from A to Z: How to go from having nothing documented (or having multiple conflicting versions) to creating a scalable, up-to-date single source of truth, all without dedicated resources. Discernment is everywhere at work if you take the time to look for it.

7.1 TAKE ACTION: Reflect:

- Where are you already applying discernment to empower your team?
- Are there other areas where you could level up and spark discernment training experiences?
- Do you observe a gap in trust, empowerment, knowledge, or resources?
- Is there a simple trial you can set up to test a roadmap like this?

The discernment training program does not exist to build skills. Reliable discernment provides outcomes that will exponentially impact your team's results.

CHAPTER 8

TRAINING

Learning that works isn't read, it's lived.

You've sat through those days when new hires shuffle into a conference room, coffee in hand, and leave three hours later, wondering what just happened. Slides were shown, jargon was thrown around, and no one ever quite figured out how it applied to their job. You've seen underperformers quietly slip through the cracks and subject-matter experts struggle to onboard new teammates. It doesn't have to be this way.

What if training felt less like a chore and more like a launchpad—where curiosity sparks action, and every exercise lands with real-world impact? In these pages, you'll discover how to turn passive learners into active explorers; how to weave empowerment into every module; and how to replace one-size-fits-all decks with tailored journeys that sing to each individual's learning style. Get ready to reinvent training as a culture-building, performance-igniting force.

Working with groups ranging from two to ten thousand, it is not a surprise to notice **training can be optimized further.** In every organization I've stepped into, training could be materially improved. My observation is that this is because, time and again, training is the last department on the priority list to see the sunlight of organizational support. Transformation of culture requires investment in training.

Here we discuss how to transition underperformers to **high performers** and ways to build new hires into subject matter experts, at the same time integrating them into the team.

A key objective is to pull new team members into an **empowered state** quickly. With reactive training programs, this is not possible. Once you have developed a proactive approach, you can begin to deploy it as early as the hiring process.

IN PRACTICE: During the interview, I paint the picture around our training. "When you join our organization, we're not going to lecture you. We're not going to overwhelm you with PowerPoint slides. We will provide the information, create a learning framework, and give you access to the necessary resources. You'll also be paired with a mentor and a training coordinator for support. But here's the deal: I expect you to come in with the biggest ladle you can find. And I want you to delve into the training material and absorb the knowledge. Don't wait for us. If you're ready for more, dig in. Ask us where to look. We'll give you all the empowerment you need, and we'll clearly explain how it works. We'll also have regular check-ins along the way."

By doing this, I'm setting the tone early: "How you approach training will determine your experience. Don't expect us to be solely responsible for your training outcome. Yes, it's on us to provide the foundation and the resources—that's our responsibility as an organization. But it's on *you* to show up ready to learn, prepared to take action."

Nurturing Active Learners

I'm looking for **active learners**, not passive. So again, my goal is to bring them into an empowered state as soon as possible. How do we do that? Starting with the interview (in Chapter 3), we connect to **critical success factors** and **milestones**.

On day one, new hires acknowledge a document outlining those factors: five to six **high-level mandates** for the role, including purpose, significance, and the intended approach for execution. Next, they receive a **roadmap** to follow. That roadmap includes **milestones** (covered in Chapter 2). It may also include other resources, but one of the key elements is integrating into the team. If they're an individual contributor, that means embedding themselves into their department and the broader organizational culture.

Embedding into the team is the first step. Ultimately, the aspirational goal is for them to become the **go-to person** on their team. I'm not saying they *must* become that person, but I am planting the seed. I'm setting the expectation as something to strive for. I don't give a timeline for achieving it. I want them to explore, learn, and grow at their own pace, presenting it very much as a challenge.

As covered in Chapter 2, there's an expectation: **five key milestones** to be completed within six months. However, within that framework, they have freedom to move at their own pace, to modulate the accelerator or the brakes as needed. This is early discernment in practice, yet driven by organic assessment using check-ins.

We all know learners progress at different paces. Quickness doesn't always correlate with performance. Fast learners are *not* the highest performers. Your procedural learners could very well become the most effective, efficient, and high-performing team members, perhaps the standard for the team.

When you set a fixed time for training—the common approach, often driven by budget or volume constraints—it can end up being tone-deaf to how people actually learn, to say nothing of unforeseen systemic issues. It overlooks the fact that individuals learn at different speeds and need varying repetitions in specific modalities. While the set time may be enough for some, it won't be enough for others. And as a result, you risk losing a potential contributor who could have been an excellent performer simply because they weren't given the time they needed to succeed, or worse, holding back a great employee who is ready to move faster than the scope allows.

Through organic assessments and check-ins, you help team members understand their current standing, where they're progressing quickly, or falling behind. If they are struggling, you can discuss factors, identify roadblocks, and support them in overcoming each challenge.

A hallmark is to provide access to the entire training content upfront. Encourage them to follow guidelines and order, don't micromanage the process. Some complete the training path in two months, others in six or more. Don't penalize someone for being methodical. Design flexibility into the process, embracing **diversity in learning styles.** This one change can lead to building your highest-performing team. Resist spoon-fed training; inspire individuals to pull the training toward them as an early engagement check.

The more there is a shift away from a model rooted in pressure to follow prescribed scope and sequencing deadlines toward one rooted in empowerment and ownership, the more proactive your program will become. You might ask, "How do I actually do that?" or "Can it really work without traditional frameworks?" You may be thinking, *No time frame? No "finish in three days," or "by week two?"* Recall my observation about training at the beginning of this chapter: Is current training actually delivering?

Here's my answer: **Assess**. Evaluate your current training. What's working? What's not? What's not working as well as it needs to? Examine which milestones are being met and which ones are causing difficulties. Then dive deeper. Ask questions, gather feedback, analyze root causes, and start solving from there. You may find that a training method based on empowerment and ownership yields the best results. Are you AI curious? Consider whether your training tech stack can be refreshed with AI-enabled technologies to bring simulated and real-world training closer together. AI tools bring new ways to streamline operational workflows; simplifying repetitive tasks, allowing reflective thinking space and time, redefining the balance of challenging, yet rewarding work. If you're unsure where to begin, start small. Choose a less critical, lower-risk area of work and run an A/B test. Give it enough time to produce measurable outcomes. You might be surprised by how well it works. We have resources on the PangeaEffect.com website to aid you in beginning this process.

Training Design

Training isn't theoretical. It's practical, best rooted in **real-world applications**. Train with case studies. Train through role-play. Train hands-on. If your team will face pressure, train under pressure. Recreate true-role scenarios. Follow up with your team regularly. Trust them, but verify their proficiency. Ensure the training is effective *for them*. Training is an opportunity to deliver learning as an immersive experience.

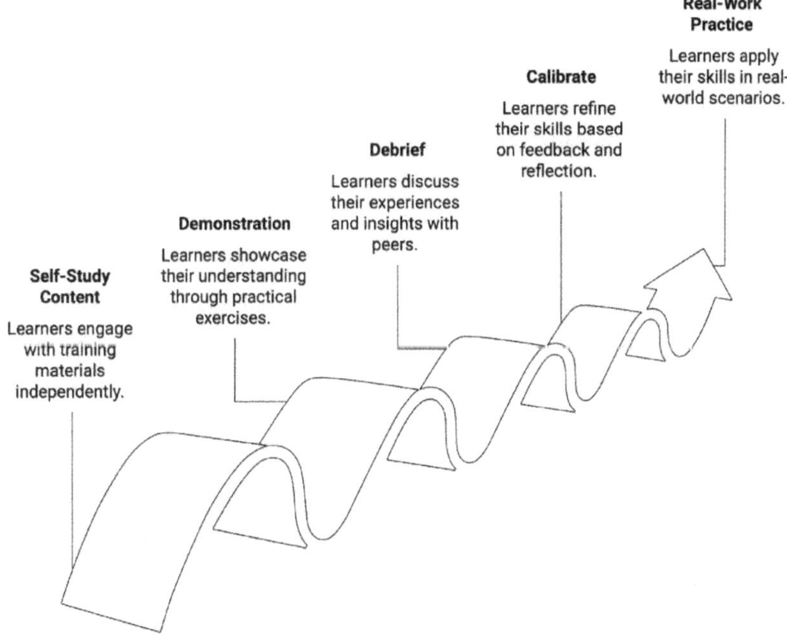

The more your training supports diverse learning styles, the more successful your outcomes will be. Be a solutionist, and bring that mindset into your training design. Still not seeing a path? Identify an ally in instructional design or develop one.

Now, you might be wondering: *If there's no strict deadline and learners are expected to find information rather than having everything pushed to them, how do I know they've absorbed the right material?* That's where **guided exploration** comes in. Provide them with content to study and use **scavenger hunts** as a learning tool. These are especially effective when learning systems incorporate where information lives and how workflows function.

For example, a scavenger hunt might involve a real-life use case: a customer who can't log into the system. Or it could be an internal employee facing the same issue. The exercise would ask:

- Do you know where to direct the user to help them log in?
- Can you guide me through the process of resetting a password?
- Can you locate the proper steps and resources?

In this way, learners gain practical experience while navigating real problems, learning where to go, what to do, and how to do it correctly. There is no separation between training materials and operational resources.

Having team members document the correct steps is valuable, and numerous excellent online training systems and tools are available. You can use everything from platforms like Kahoot, which gamify training through quizzes and point-based engagement, to more robust, structured systems designed for in-depth training delivery. The key is to measure progress.

For example, how long did it take them to complete the scavenger hunt? How successful were they? Did they complete all the steps? There are multiple facets of learning embedded in that process.

Within each module (content upfront, along with a recommended order for completing it), there are clear steps and milestones. At the end of each one, provide an exercise and demonstration opportunity to ensure they've grasped the key takeaways. You can gamify it to make it more engaging, or keep it straightforward with a basic quiz. That's your **quantitative data,** confirmation that they've learned what they need to know. As a responsibility, these steps can fall to a shared or dedicated resource such as a training coordinator. I've had success adding this to a developing leader's role.

All together, this is the **mastery learning cycle:** Self-study content, demonstration, debrief, calibrate, and engage in real-work practice. Soon after hire, a small percentage of each day is spent engaging in actual work, focused on frequent and simple use cases. As confidence builds naturally, the percentage of real-work time expands until it becomes the full day, needing less and less support along the way.

Also employed are debriefs with colleagues and supervisors. When training isn't isolated in a silo, and new hires interact with existing team members throughout the process, they emerge more connected and better integrated into the team. That also creates a stronger support system for both the new hire and the existing team. All of this contributes to a more effective, measurable, and empowering training experience.

8.1 TAKE ACTION: Build Training That Delivers

1. **Audit and Listen.** Start with the truth. What's working? What's slowing people down? Talk to recent hires and remove what's in the way.

2. **Map the Path.** Define clear milestones from onboarding to proficiency. Focus on progress, not time. People move faster when the destination is visible.

3. **Design for Ownership.** Provide structure, tools, and real-world practice—then expect people to lead their own learning. Training isn't something done *to* them; it's something they do.

4. **Equip and Engage.** Mentors should be sherpas—not just pointing the way, but walking it with them. Their job is to clear obstacles, build confidence, and keep momentum.

5. **Test, Measure, Evolve.** Pilot the approach. Measure what matters: performance, not just completion. Refine fast and build out what works.

6. **Ensure Your Trainees** live your content.

CHAPTER 9

PROFICIENCY

Skill gaps are breakthroughs in waiting.

In practice, proficiency goes beyond mere task completion—it's the quiet confidence that lets a teammate diagnose a problem before it even lands on your desk. You'll notice it when someone sets up their own quick-reference guides, offers a shortcut that saves the whole group time, or spots a pattern that turns recurring challenges into repeatable solutions. These moments aren't random; they're the signaling of a skill set so deeply internalized that it becomes second nature.

Proficiency also thrives in collaboration. When a team member transitions from asking for help to becoming the one other seeks out, you've hit a tipping point. They're no longer just executing instructions; they're co-authoring best practices. That ripple effect—where one person's mastery elevates the entire group—is the hallmark of a cultivated culture.

Just as a mature garden produces more than fruit—its blossoms attract pollinators; its soil nourishes future growth—proficient individuals enrich your organization in ways you can't always capture on a spreadsheet. Their impact shows up in faster problem-solving, stronger peer coaching, and a self-sustaining cycle of continuous improvement. That's the true measure of proficiency—and the legacy you want to plant.

Achieving Proficiency

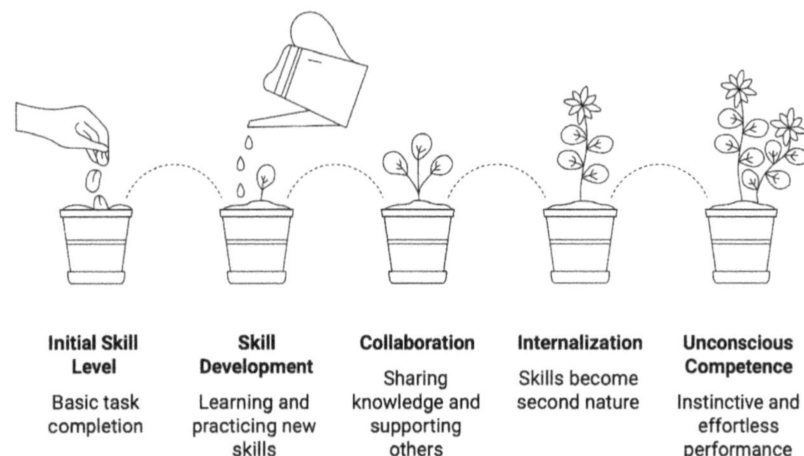

Proficiency is a measure of the level of healthy productivity. You will observe the fruits of your efforts by cataloging the skills an employee brings to their day-to-day work:

- demonstrating skills to others (engagement)
- knowing when to ask for help
- offering support where needed
- being a contributing team member
- demonstrating unconscious competence
- enabling the team to reach proficiency
- collaborating in a meaningful way

Add your own metrics, aligned to your team. All show qualitative data points that indicate proficiency.

Unconscious competence: You may be unfamiliar with this term. It refers to a stage of mastery where tasks are performed correctly, accurately, and on time—***instinctively*** and **effortlessly**, *without* conscious thought.

So what might this look like? Imagine a well-seasoned driver preparing to take a left—do they think, *I'm going to turn on the blinker, I'm going to turn left* every single time? Or do they know where they're going and instinctively turn on the blinker as they prepare to turn left? They don't think about it; they just do it.

Measuring Proficiency

There are many methods and tools available to make proficiency a measurable aspect of productivity. Examples include survey scores, response time, resolution rate, sales conversion, or error rate. Consider the team's relationship with each metric:

- Does it generate improvements, or is it simply punitive?
- Is a healthy dynamic for self-reflection and development present?
- Does proficiency build trust in the metric?
- Does each metric highlight actual performance?
- Is there clear alignment of top performers with high scores and low performers as outliers?

If not, you might experience resistance and need to recalibrate. Keep in mind that proficiency shows up as the result of foundational work, or nutrients in the soil of your garden, intended to set teams up for success. Proficiency is an **output,** known as a **lag measure**. **Lead measures** are the preparation or input that influences the outcomes you are striving to achieve. In training, lead measures could include pre-assessments, check-ins, scavenger hunt–style activities, and other performance indicators embedded in the work. If these lead measures show high pass rates, the individual is more likely to reach proficiency, as a lag measure, quickly. If pass rates are low, proficiency is a less likely output.

If proficiency, as a lag measure, represents the output you're aiming for: capable, confident team members operating with excellence, this can be measured using both **soft and hard metrics (**qualitative and quantitative data).

Check in to see your culture in action. Are there flowers or weeds? Do you need to water with development? Is the sunlight shining on your garden? How many blooms of culture do you observe each day? This is all a reflection of current culture against the backdrop of proficiency.

IN PRACTICE: In a call center, it is essential that agents handle situations with poise and confidence, communicating clearly and professionally. As a leader, you prepare the agents to bridge their proficiency gaps with certain skills. One such skill is an **exit strategy.**

What does that look like? It could be as simple as saying, "Let me connect with my expert and get back to you by the end of the day with an update." This response instills confidence. It demonstrates professionalism, self-awareness, and a desire to serve.

Pre-proficiency, they build discernment to recognize when to apply this skill. Adoption, as a **lead measure**, is a high indicator of both agent confidence and customer satisfaction within the novice gap. The frequency with which they deploy this strategy (**lead)** can be measured against your service levels (**lag**).

A key leadership responsibility is creating an environment where asking for help is seen as a strength, not a weakness. Empowered team members speak up when they hit a limit, knowing they'll be supported.

Whether a new team member is working in spreadsheets, following a workflow, or capturing another specialized task, they need both the knowledge to do so, and the confidence to seek help when the task is beyond them. When evaluating performance, ask: *Do they have an exit strategy?*

As leaders, we must identify gaps in proficiency and work to close them. Do you expect employees to resolve things on their own? Do you equip them with the critical tools, knowledge, resources, and internal advocates? How might your set-up risk undermine high performers?

Without proper support, even top contributors disengage due to a lack of autonomy. This leads to frustration and reduced productivity. Along the way, they could become detractors, add management friction, and become unplanned attrition. Ask yourself: *Did it need to come to that? Was I engaged enough to notice the decline in performance? Did I initiate the proper support in time?*

Finally, proficiency requires **performance confirmation.** Metrics could include service levels, financial outcomes, task completion speed, or defect rate. These data points confirm whether a team member is a contributing factor to the group. There are many possible performance indicators, but the key is that they are measurable and serve as confirmation of performance.

You've nurtured your team's growth, celebrated their wins, and watched proficiency bloom like a well-tended garden. Yet even the healthiest plot can harbor a few stragglers—areas where a plant struggles for sunlight or the soil isn't quite right. As a leader, your instincts tell you when the overall harvest looks strong, but true excellence demands that you zoom in and spot the lone weeds before they spread.

In the next section, we'll sharpen our lens on identifying gaps between success and stagnation. You'll discover how to diagnose whether a shortfall is a one-off fluke or a sign of a deeper, system-wide issue—and how to close those gaps with both empathy and precision. Let's turn that rising tide into a sweeping wave that lifts every boat.

Identifying Gaps

Performance is assessed against baseline metrics. For individual contributors, the question becomes:

- Are they outperforming the team baseline?
- Is the team performing at or above the organizational average?
- Are they raising the bar?
- Has the tipping point been reached, so that overall performance improves?

In short, a rising tide lifts all boats. How do we evaluate a team member's performance in relation to their team and broader program expectations? As a leader, if you're noticing a performance gap or launching a new initiative that requires a pivot, there will naturally be areas to address. A first step is identifying whether each gap is systemic or isolated.

- **Is this a systemic issue?** Does it span the organization, department, or entire team? If so, is there a lack of training, knowledge, or resources? Is the issue beyond the control of the person executing the work?

- **Is the issue isolated?** Is it limited to a specific individual or group? If it's a group, are they part of the same team? In that case, look at the team leader or the systems. If it's an individual, ask: *How can I support this person?* Is it a systems issue affecting them? Or a gap in knowledge, skills, or role fit?

Once you determine the root cause, you know where to focus. Importantly, this process does not remove ownership, accountability, or empowerment from the individual. Rather, it clears the path to ensure they have what they need to succeed. If they do have the tools, assume they're trying to do the right thing. *Assume positive intent.*

From there, figure out how best to support them in getting the right result. Consider how the person learns best, and whether they're in the right role for their strengths. These are key questions to ask yourself, and the answers will point to your next step.

- Is the goal to help them stay in the role and thrive again?
- Do they require support to regain performance parity with the rest of the team?
- Or is it time to explore whether another role in the organization might be a better fit?

CONVERSATION PLAYBOOK:

For the last option above, say: "You're a valued team member, and I want to make sure you're in a role that best supports your strengths. Would you be open to exploring other opportunities within the organization together?"

There are many ways to approach this conversation, and your communication style should adjust to align with the individual. If the team member is receptive and coachable, a collaborative discussion may be a suitable approach. If they are resistant, combative, or unwilling to engage in coaching, consider a more structured and direct approach. Either way, it's your responsibility to assess fit and offer support if a change is needed.

Judging, Assessing, and Providing Step Goals

Let's talk about **judging and assessing** for a moment. We all do it. It's human nature.

Once we judge or assess something, we assign meaning to it. We are meaning-making machines. Over the years, you've continually absorbed information and turned that information (data points) into meaning. The meaning you assign becomes the lens through which you view a situation. It shapes your perception, your conclusions, and your actions.

Think of the meaning as a filter—like sunglasses tinting. Dark brown lenses can dim a bright and colorful day. In reality, nothing outside changed. Switching to an amber-hued set has things take on a warmer feel, the contrast pops, and there's a rosy glow.

This mirrors our perceptions and, if ignored, can color our approach. When we process data or absorb information, we do so through a lens, our **perspective.** Our experiences, history, and beliefs shape this. We're not going to unpack all of that here; that's another book for another day, maybe even by another author. But here's what I *do* want you to consider: When you're speaking with a team member, what lens are you wearing? Can you remove the glasses entirely and see the person in front of you as they are, without assumptions, without judgment? Can you seek to understand before trying to be understood?

So, how do you do that? You learn through discovery. You lead with curiosity. Approach with a hypothesis—but don't attach your ego to it. You might think, *I believe there's a seventy percent chance it'll go this way, and a thirty percent chance it'll go another way.* That's fine.

But here's the hard part: Give up the need to be right. Let go of terms like "better." Why? Because terms like *better, more,* and *fewer* aren't measurable. They're vague. A few might be many different amounts. We interpret these words individually.

Now, I'm not saying the world is black and white. There's a spectrum. There are grays, colors, and nuances, but using vague, subjective terms weakens our communication. It takes away power from what we're trying to accomplish. So I encourage you to be specific. Use measurable terms. Provide concrete metrics to aim for. Assess where someone is, not where they should be, or used to be, or could be, but where they *are* right now. Then, work with them to create an aspirational goal.

Create a clear, measurable **step goal** to help the individual move in the right direction. As we discussed in earlier chapters, the goal is to build winning momentum, the **flywheel of success**. So ask yourself: *How can I give them a meaningful step forward that also meets the business's needs without causing harm?*

Of course, if the performance gap is large enough to harm the company, then a more significant improvement is needed. That's a different situation entirely. In those cases, it's essential to be transparent, direct, and honest.

A good leader is willing to return to the foundation to build a skyscraper where a two-story building once stood. If the foundation isn't solid, you can only build so high before everything collapses. You can only drive so much performance and reach a certain level of executional excellence. Sometimes, the best path forward is to step back, especially if you're far off course, the team is underperforming, and the business is demanding change. That's when you need transformation.

These are opportunities to take a close look and ask: Where are we strong? Where are we performing well? Start there. Build from a place of proficiency. If you're strong in one area, return to that strength and rebuild from there.

You may now be asking: What are better alternatives to vague terms like *better*, *fewer*, *more*, or *less*? What's measurable is a number, a percentage, a timeframe, a concrete result, or a level of satisfaction, all of which can be captured using tangible indicators. Whether it's numerical ratings, percentages, or even visual cues like smiley faces, what matters is that the metric is clear and trackable. It should be immediately apparent whether success was achieved.

CONVERSATION PLAYBOOK:

If you need to speak with a team member whose performance isn't meeting expectations: "I've been reviewing the team's performance and have two areas of focus. I wanted to talk through some of what's been happening with you in relation to these areas. First, I will show you what I've observed and invite you to share your take on it, because I value your perspective."

Working from the report itself, whatever form the data takes, I encourage them to speak honestly about what they see in their work.

They may respond in various ways:

- "I'm looking at it, but I'm not sure what you're asking."
- "Yeah, I reviewed my work. Aside from this small issue, everything looks fine to me."
- They might get defensive: "I always do everything right."
- **Or, ideally, they might say:** "Now that I'm looking at it, I realize I hadn't reflected on how I was doing things. But I can see now that I could have handled this differently to get the result we were aiming for."

That last response is the goal. That's **ownership**. When someone can reflect on their performance, identify where they went wrong, and speak with clarity and confidence about how they'll improve, that's **self-coaching**. That's integrity. That's recommitment.

If they've recognized it themselves: "Okay, great. Now that we've recognized this, I'm seeing that the number of widgets you produced today—the volume of work—is thirty percent lower than the rest of the team. Was there something about the work you were assigned that might explain the lower output? Did something happen? Was it a specific type of task?"

I **assume positive intent** and give them space to respond.

They might say: "I ran into a technical issue and spent an hour with IT support. It was frustrating, but once it was resolved, I got right back to work." **Or:** "No, it was a pretty average day."

If you see they're usually in line with the team (within a known performance range), respond: "Your usual output is consistently on par with the team."

If nothing stands out about the day in question, add: "When do you expect to be back at goal, back at par with the rest of the team?"

I ask this intentionally because I want them to self-identify the next step. I want them to own it. I could say, "I expect you to be back at par by the end of the week," or "by tomorrow," or "by next month." But if I do that, I take all the power away from them. Now, I'm imposing a deadline instead of giving them the opportunity to commit to one themselves.

Sometimes, I do have to set that expectation, but I don't need to start there.

Instead, lead with: "I trust you. Something happened, and I'm not going to focus on that. What I care about now is what you're going to do next and after that. Let's focus on the future."

Give them space to create a plan. You've already done the work of identifying what happened; you've pulled those weeds. Now it's time to fertilize and water. It's time to empower them, to focus on what's ahead, and to support them in moving forward.

Then, stand for them to come up with a clear timeframe. If they don't, there's a gap. And that's when you listen carefully for what's *not* being said. There's something underneath that silence that needs to be explored. As a leader, it's our job to help uncover that in a way that's safe for that employee to be able to share what's present for them.

9.1 TAKE ACTION: Build for Proficiency

1. **Define what proficiency looks like.** Make it visible and measurable. Use real work, real metrics, and real feedback. Clarity wins.

2. **Track lead measures.** Don't wait for performance to lag before stepping in. Use assessments, check-ins, and milestone reviews to keep people moving toward proficiency early.

3. **Normalize asking for help.** Create a culture where seeking clarity or support is a sign of strength, not weakness. Proficient teams lift each other.

4. **Address gaps, not just people.** If someone's struggling, ask whether the issue is systemic or individual. Then solve it from there. Never confuse a leadership failure with a talent problem.

5. **Coach forward.** When performance slips, stay curious. Lead with data, hold space for ownership, and guide them to the next step. Don't assign a deadline—invite a commitment.

If you have been counting skill gaps, start measuring breakthroughs.

CHAPTER 10

ENGAGEMENT

If engagement is not the priority, mediocrity becomes the standard.

You've laid the groundwork—clear expectations, seamless access to resources, and a culture of continuous learning—and you've watched proficiency bloom across your team. Yet even the most finely tuned engine needs fuel to keep running. Engagement is that spark: the energy that transforms skills into passion, tasks into purpose, and routines into breakthroughs.

In the pages ahead, we'll explore how to kindle genuine engagement so that every team member moves not because they have to, but because they want to. You'll learn how to tap into the unique motivations of each person, create feedback loops that feel less like checklists and more like conversations, and build rituals that bind your people together. Engagement isn't a reward—it's the oxygen your high-performing culture breathes. Let's dive in and set your team alight.

Engagement is the pivot point.

This is the culmination of what we've covered in this book so far. We have brought everyone to a place where they are now performing at their highest level. Now, we can figure out how to take them from where they are and have them open their minds and catch a new vision—to perform at a level that is unreasonable, at a level of the unexpected, at a level beyond anyone's imagination.

There may be many step goals required to reach the larger objective, but the idea is to take your team as far as you can and then push the limit as one. Ask: *Is there something else that can change? Is it within our control?* Focus on what's inside your sphere of influence. That's what it means to be an engaged leader: acknowledging your team as high-performing individuals and calling on them to keep challenging themselves. This helps them grow, develop, and stay engaged in work that remains interesting and meaningful.

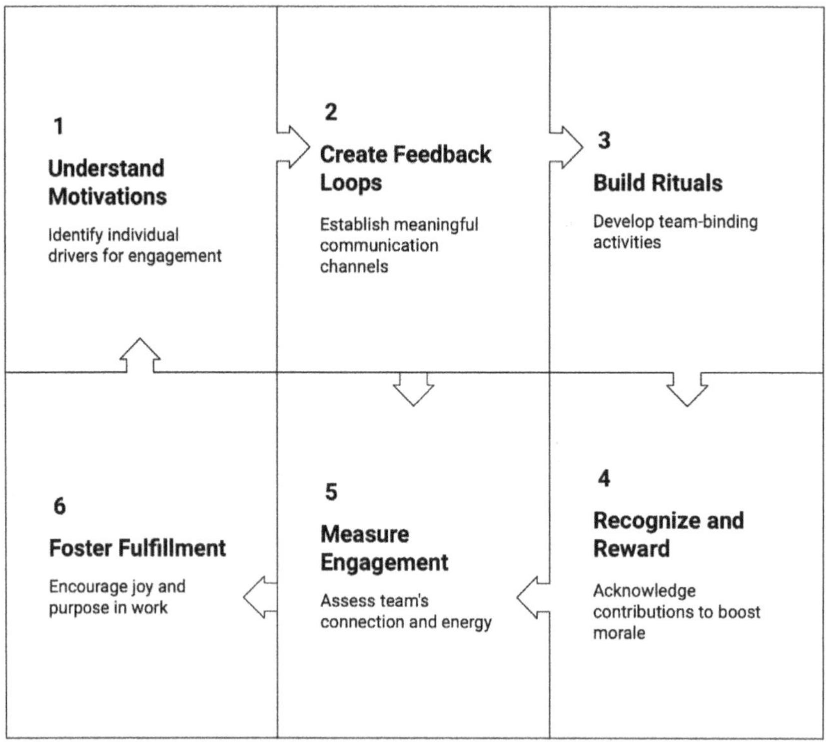

Providing Recognition

A key part of engagement is finding ways to **recognize** and **reward** people so they stay motivated and connected. Acknowledging, "You corrected three errors before they were submitted. That saved us hours. Thank you." Or, "Your consistent performance has impressed me and made a huge difference. I appreciate you showing us what is possible." Stay specific to an accomplishment and measurable with data. General feedback is empty.

Know who thrives on public and private acknowledgements. Find the best method for each. One simple way is to check in on the feedback from your feedback, and keep adjusting to what speaks to them.

- Handwritten note
- Personalized gift
- Sot bonus
- Certificate or Plaque

The key is: You have to know your people. Incorporate a questionnaire to inform these future moments:

New Hire Questionnaire	
• What's your favorite food? • Is there a book or podcast that has really influenced you? • What is your top pick for a restaurant?	• Best movie? • If you were to be recognized for an accomplishment, what would that look like to you?

That feedback becomes invaluable. Asking what motivates and inspires them will guide you on ways to keep them engaged. If you observe disengagement, leverage this for best results.

Maintaining Engagement

Engagement is where meaningful **measurement** begins.

Connection to the organization is inherent to engagement. When missing, leaders provide the nutrients of reconnecting people to their career path and the team's larger performance goals. Examine the environment by asking: "What have we done (or not done) to cultivate engagement?"

- Do we offer clear career pathing?
- Are there opportunities for growth and development?
- Are there chances for them to contribute in different areas of the organization?
- Are they working inside their skills and strengths?
- Where else can I look deeply for these opportunities?

IN PRACTICE: While overseeing the transformational project at the call center where I devised the North Star principles, another outcome of my **listening roadshow** was a surprising one. The questions I asked of the leaders were along the lines of:

- What does success look like for their department and mine?
- What matters most to them between the two?
- What do they expect from our team to support their efforts?

In one case, both the CFO and the controller responded with remarkably similar language. That was a good sign; there was alignment. They said they needed to know that I, as a leader, was owning financial responsibility and that I would hold myself accountable, so they wouldn't have to. And that was what mattered most to the business.

I thought about that for a long time. At first, I figured it was a pretty standard task for a leader: Manage the budget, and manage it well. But I saw an opportunity to take it a step further:

I incorporated a "financial accountability" metric into our North Star principles.

Initially, I was questioned quite heavily, especially around the concept of the frontline contributing to this as a metric. You might question it as well. It may sound shocking.

How can you do that at the frontline level? There are so many factors that impact finances at the organizational or departmental level. How can you bring that down to an individual frontline team member, someone whose salary is fixed, who is hourly? You already know what their labor cost will be.

And that's true. However, in a call center environment, **schedule adherence**—being present when you're scheduled, on time, every time—is critical. So is returning from breaks on time. Why? Because when you have 700 people in the same role, and 200 of them are fifteen minutes late from lunch or break, each thinking it's no big deal, the business starts to suffer. If everyone's doing it, we can't answer customer calls, respond to emails, or handle other communications in time. That directly impacts service levels, customer experience, and yes—it costs the company money. There's an **ROI** (Return on Investment) cost to that.

Furthermore, the awareness a frontline team has when this is part of the mission-critical components allows training, management, and coaching to address wins and opportunities related to double work, impacts on other departments, and "in-the-moment" choices. This detail can set the team apart.

Another application encourages holistic awareness from the individual expanding out.

IN PRACTICE: Attrition was high, and I couldn't rely on the team to consistently show up. That required me to hire twenty more people just to maintain coverage and service levels. That comes with real, measurable costs:

- Recruiting
- Onboarding
- Training
- Time to proficiency
- Time to value

Based on our supervisor-to-agent ratio, we needed an additional supervisor. Our trainer's capacity was stretched, and the quality team had to evaluate even more calls or emails. The downstream cost added up quickly.

Now, I wasn't going to explain all of that to a frontline agent who's just trying to do their job on the phone. But I did set clear, reasonable expectations: "My expectation is that your schedule adherence is at ninety-eight percent. My expectation is that you return from breaks on time ninety-eight percent of the time." Setting it at one hundred percent would be setting them up for failure. That's not productive. It doesn't support our bigger goal of team cohesion, a thriving culture, and employee engagement. If goals are unrealistic or unattainable over time, people just disengage. Set expectations at a level that's challenging, yet achievable. Drive ownership of their part.

I never tell an agent, "Hey, when you were late, we had to hire two new people, and it cost us [X] dollars." That's not the conversation I'm having with them. I might have that conversation with a peer leader or my finance team when the impact is significant enough. With team members, I focus on behaviors. If they manage those well (if they're present, reliable, and engaged), we can reinvest in the business. We can enhance their work experience, provide better tools and resources, and contribute to job stability by maintaining the company's financial health. And those are things that resonate with almost everyone in the organization.

Engagement is connecting the dots from the biggest picture to the most granular level and then zooming back out again. Did you recognize the zooming-in effect I just demonstrated in practice? If you didn't, I encourage you to go back and read it again. See if you pick up on how I started at the biggest picture: What did the CFO and controller require from my department? Then I brought it down to that frontline team member's specific behavior that I'm looking for, something measurable. And then I zoomed back out again.

And when I did that, everyone was tuned into the same radio station: **WIIFM—What's In It For Me?** At the end of the day, they're asking: "Why is this important? What's in it for me if I meet these goals?"

Here's what's in it for them:

- The company is in a healthier position.
- There's a job opportunity because we can reinvest and grow the business.
- We don't have to over-hire, which frees up our time to better support existing team members and focus on giving them what they need.

There are numerous powerful ways to tell this story, ways that inspire and excite people to contribute.

Monitoring Fulfillment

We can't end a discussion on engagement and its measurement without covering **fulfillment**. Fulfillment shows up in many ways. Are your team members—and you— energized? If someone has a naturally downbeat demeanor, do they still stay fully engaged in the work? Do they talk about going home and sharing something they accomplished at work? Do they mention learning something new? These are all signs of fulfillment. So yes, it can be measured, but it requires mindfulness and thoughtful observation.

Imagine fulfillment as the secret ingredient that turns hard work into joy—like discovering the perfect seasoning that makes every bite memorable. When fulfillment is alive on your team, you'll feel it in the spontaneous "aha" moments, the quick-fire problem solving, and the casual corridor chats that spark brilliant ideas.

Another question to consider as a path to fulfillment: Are you and your team working to your strengths? As a young leader, I believed my job was to help people reach the highest level of performance. I thought the best way to do that was to fix their weaknesses. After all, their strengths were already there; they'd take care of themselves, right? But I found that I was working hard and seeing minimal results. Occasionally, someone would break through, but it was rare.

Over time, I learned that it's far more effective to identify and invest in a person's strengths. Sometimes, those strengths are apparent right away. If you hire someone for an analytics role, they will be skilled at pulling data together and synthesizing it. If someone has been building widgets for years, they'll need to learn your way of doing it, but they already know the basics. You don't need to teach them *what* to do—just *how* you do it here.

So the real question becomes: Which of their strengths are underutilized? Where can they lean in even more deeply? How can you help them tap into that zone of confidence and engagement? When people operate in their strengths, they feel empowered. They feel energized. They think: *This is something I can really get into. This is something I can do.* Now, this doesn't mean we ignore their weaknesses, but the focus shifts.

Tie Fulfillment to Purpose

Fulfillment blossoms when daily tasks connect to something bigger. Try weaving a quick "purpose moment" into your next stand-up: ask each person to name one way today's work advanced the team's mission. Those thirty seconds anchor routine tasks in real impact, and remind everyone why they showed up.

Create "Fulfillment Check-Ins"

Beyond annual surveys, introduce ultra-short, two-question pulses:

What part of your work this week energized you most?

What's one thing you'd tweak to make your day more impactful?

Rotate who reviews and shares themes each week. When people see their feedback shape real changes—like tweaking meeting lengths or adjusting project scopes—they'll feel heard and invested.

Build a Harvest Wall

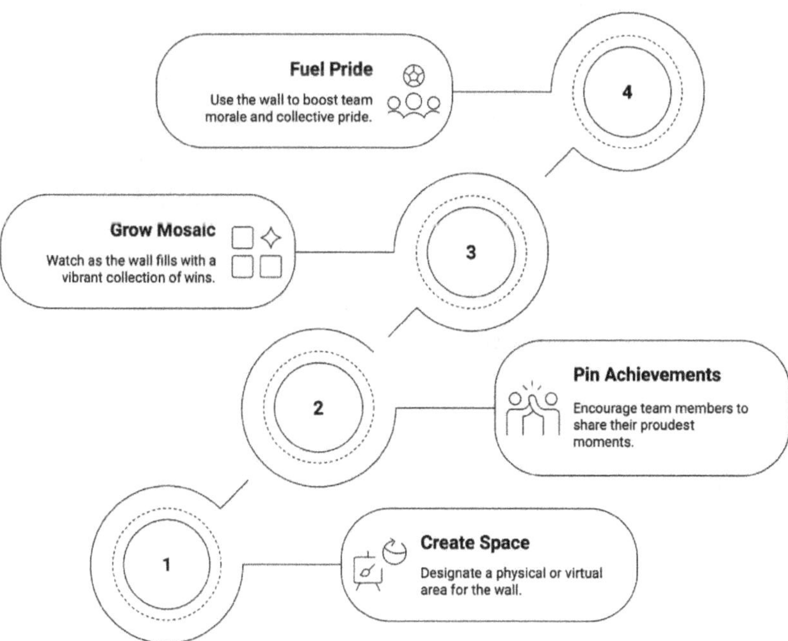

Turn your physical or virtual whiteboard into a "Harvest Wall" where team members pin their proudest achievements—big or small. A quick note about a streamlined process, a customer shout-out, or a personal breakthrough all belong here. Over time, the wall becomes a vibrant mosaic of wins that fuels collective pride.

Link Fulfillment to Growth

I apply the **80/20 rule**: Eighty percent of my time and energy are devoted to helping them utilize their strengths to drive performance. Twenty percent is spent on areas of opportunity. That time is focused on development, helping them navigate the weaknesses that might be holding them back. We look at those gaps, address them, and support their growth.

Weaknesses I've addressed as opportunities include:

- Getting flustered easily when things become stressful
- Low energy early in the day impacting the team
- Inconsistent time to task completion

Use your 80/20 rule not just for strengths but for stretch goals. Encourage people to pick one "moonshot" challenge each quarter—something that nudges them just beyond their comfort zone. When they succeed or even move the needle, you'll watch fulfillment soar as they realize they're capable of more than they imagined.

Model Vulnerability and Curiosity

Fulfillment thrives in cultures where it's safe to be human. Share your own "midweek moment of joy"—perhaps a small victory in a personal project or an insight you gained from a difficult conversation. Your openness signals that fulfillment isn't just a checkbox; it's an ongoing, shared adventure.

Celebrate the Unseen

Often, fulfillment hides in the mundane: the hours spent refining a slide deck, the late-night email that resolved a crisis, or the quiet coaching that helped a peer finally "get it." Spot those moments and shine a light on them. A brief mention in a team email or a personal note can turn an overlooked effort into a badge of honor.

Fulfillment as Fuel for Resilience

High fulfillment acts like a shock absorber for stress. When unexpected hurdles appear—missed deadlines, shifting priorities—a team rooted in fulfillment bounces back. They've internalized that their work matters, so setbacks feel like detours, not dead ends.

IN PRACTICE: "Drive-bys," once referred to as **Manage by Walking Around** (MBWA), also go by side-by-side, shadowing, or check-ins. Works remotely and in person.

Observe how focused or distracted someone is on their work. If it's a one-off, let it go. But a pattern warrants follow-up. "I am checking to make sure everything's going well, and see if you need anything."

They will be open, curious, deflective, or disengaged. For each scenario, adjust accordingly.

It is less about what you say and more about generating a meaningful interaction for both of you. Focus on the pattern and seek context. Explain your observations and the perceptions that you are investigating. End with "Are you in a good place? Tell me about what I am seeing." This opens up for an actual conversation.

It's a trust-but-verify methodology to assess engagement.

Another engagement tool is **skip-levels**. A skip-level is where you meet with the team of your direct reports. The focus will be on building rapport. Keep it light and focus on relationships. At some point, "How often do you think it makes sense for us to meet?" It's an assessment. It could be an indicator of engagement. You can always use the skip-level cadence that they drive as a temperature check on engagement related to what they are working on.

Some people crave structure, while others require flexibility. When checking in, it needs to be in support of what you know about *them.* It can't be from your perspective alone. "Tell me what it's like to walk in your shoes." If you're empathetic, they'll pick up on that.

10.1 TAKE ACTION: Use observation to monitor engagement. Leverage check-ins and drive-bys. Powerful conversations can uncover deeper issues that are affecting engagement.

When was the last time you had a powerful conversation, one that could uncover deeper issues affecting someone's engagement? It helps you see the whole person and the bigger picture. Schedule two skip levels in the next two weeks and three drive-bys on your calendar.

If this chapter has achieved its goal, you have a new priority that will be a mediocrity-busting endeavor to take on. Are you up for the challenge?

CHAPTER 11

INNOVATION AND IMPLEMENTATION

Not All Strengths Are Created Equal

Have you ever watched a spark of genius ignite in a brainstorming session, only to see it fade away into meeting minutes and forgotten to-dos? Every great breakthrough begins with an idea, but far too many of those sparks sputter out before they ever become reality. That's why this chapter matters more than any other: it's where vision meets action, and where creativity earns its wings.

Here, you'll discover how to shepherd raw ideas through the messy middle—transforming them from loose musings into concrete plans that your team can rally around. You'll learn to spot the moments when an idea needs room to breathe, when it needs a push to the finish line, and how to balance the dreamers and doers on your squad. By the end, you won't just have a toolbox for innovation—you'll have a roadmap for implementation that honors every insight you've gathered so far. Let's turn those brilliant "what ifs" into "what's next."

Whether you're an **innovator**, an **implementer**, or a **maintainer**, you'll find support in this chapter.

Our differences are strengths. For me, building a business and a team lights me up. For others, it's being a **promoter**—talking about the business, sharing, and influencing others to get involved, such as sales teams. For some, it's **operations**—completing the work with integrity, as defined earlier in the book.

Identify who *you* are. And, just as importantly, identify who your team members are. A well-designed team has a few hallmarks:

A balance of diverse strengths: A **promoter** who lights up the team, bringing energy and joy. The **analyzer** who enjoys gathering data and providing insights. **Creators** are your brainstorm ideators. Know your **executors–** they will implement.

Alignment to the department goals: It's elemental to see analysts flock to technical areas, creatives to marketing, and promoters to sales, just be sure to find the diversity within these regions so your teams are not hindered by being lopsided or too homogenous.

Mind the gap: Seek out and amplify the key archetypes without which results are at risk. It's a hard truth to realize, but if your team lacks a natural or developed player with innovation and implementation strengths, leaders will need to take decisive action to close this gap.

If you have a good mix of these traits across your team, yet are missing a natural, developed, or adaptive innovator, take a look and ask yourself: *Would adding someone like this to my team make a difference? Would it help us work smarter, not harder?* The reason is that innovation is constantly evolving, and innovators are naturally tuned into the nature of business.

The guide that follows outlines the key archetypes for building high-performing, well-balanced teams:

Team Strength Archetypes: Quick Reference

"The reasonable man adapts himself to the world: the unreasonable one persists in trying to adapt the world to himself. Therefore, all progress depends on the unreasonable man."
—George Bernard Shaw, Nobel Prize–winning playwright

Role	Core Strength	Value to the Team	What They Need
Builder	Initiative & momentum	Starts from scratch, drives progress in ambiguity	Freedom to create and quick decision cycles
Creator	Concept & originality	Generates compelling content, solutions, or products	Clear direction with room to explore and refine
Innovator	Vision & ideas	Sparks breakthroughs and creative leaps	Space to explore and early involvement
Promoter	Energy & influence	Inspires buy-in, drives momentum	Visibility, audience, and delivery partners
Challenger	Constructive friction	Questions groupthink, surfaces blind spots	Psychological safety and leadership backing
Executor	Precision & follow-through	Delivers outcomes, drives project closure	Milestones, ownership, and accountability
Implementer	Execution & structure	Builds systems, delivers consistent results	Clear goals, timelines, and autonomy

Tactician	Accuracy & consistency	Protects quality, ensures precision	Focus time, defined scope, and clarity
Integrator	Alignment & connection	Bridges silos, aligns teams and priorities	Cross-functional visibility and collaborative roles
Analyst	Insight & evaluation	Turns data into decisions, sees what others miss	Access to data, time to think, and space to challenge assumptions
Coach	Development & support	Elevates others through feedback and mentorship	Time with people, trust, and a growth culture
Guardian	Risk-awareness & compliance	Protects integrity, enforces standards	Involvement early in decisions, access to details

Note: *Individuals may show strength in more than one area. The goal is to recognize and activate what each person brings.*

The Pyramid: Building High-Performing Teams

Consider a model I've developed for assessing, leading, transforming, and building high-performing teams.

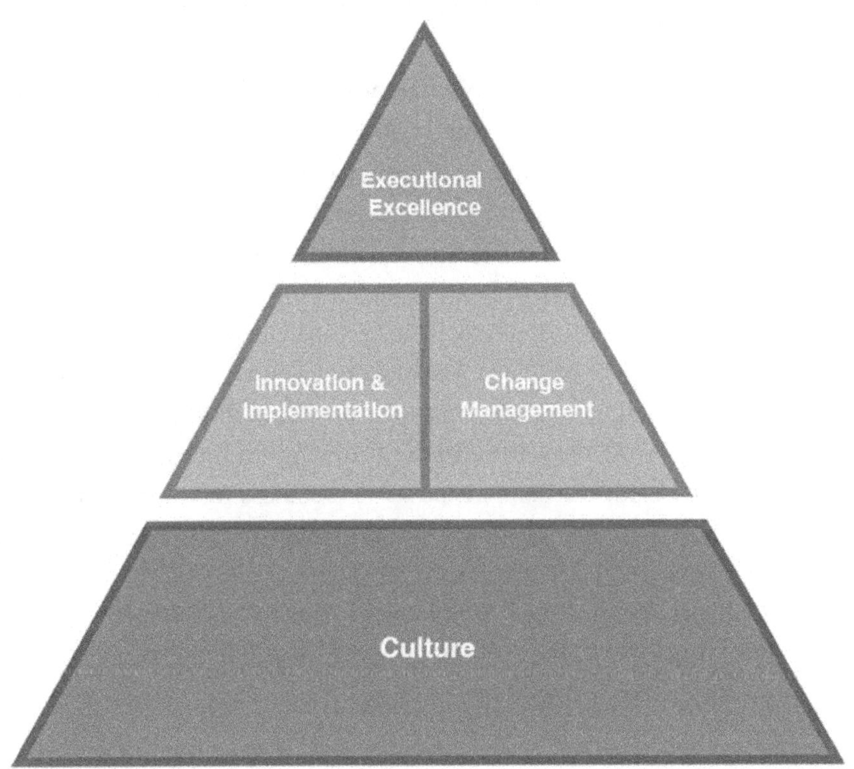

The E3 Effect™

The bottom tier is **culture**. Foundation matters. It has to be rock solid. And where there are cracks, they need to be addressed—sealed, monitored, and reinforced to ensure everything built on top of it holds fast.

The second level is divided into two sections. On the right is **change management**, which I discussed in Chapter 5. On the left is **innovation and implementation**, which is what we're discussing now.

And finally, at the very top of the pyramid is **executional excellence**. Executional excellence is where the metrics come into play. It's where the business starts gaining what it's meant to gain from your team's work.

Deep Dive: Innovation and Implementation

Let's dig into **innovation** and **implementation**. Alongside the dual purpose of change management sits the critical aspect of innovation and implementation. It is built upon the concept of engagement, because we cannot innovate and implement in a meaningful way without being engaged in the work. What matters here is that the individual is engaged enough to continually seek ways to improve the business for the greater good.

It's not about how many people you manage—it's about who's on your team. Whether you're leading a small group or overseeing multiple teams across the organization, your team benefits from having an **innovator**—someone who consistently brings ideas that move the business forward. From there, seek out the complementary strength: an **implementer** to drive execution.

Innovation occurs in all sizes. It could show up as matching a field in a tool to the term used internally. or speak to a groundbreaking tactic that revolutionizes the entire operation.

Look for these key insights:

- Are they engaged in the right areas for current focus or needs?
- Are they zeroed in on what will move the needle—for the business, the department, the team, or even for themselves?
- Is their idea one that will genuinely make a difference?

Welcoming innovators' ideas takes a management system; a proven framework helps sift through the elicited and captured sparks, prioritize them, and feed the implementers.

IN PRACTICE: Create a standardized structure for ideas to live and take flight.

1. **Organizing the Framework**– Kanban Boards in tools like *Trello* or *Jira* are simple and effective. A Kanban is a system of columns set up by topics. Under each column, you create cards, each representing a specific idea. Within each card, you can include detailed information, workflows, and other customizable elements.

    a. Name columns based on value to operational goals. Defining this collaboratively is another exercise in all the things that are becoming part of your high-performing team playbook– discernment, engagement, consensus building.

    - **Low-value** is infrequent (less than once a month), low cost and impacting a small subset of stakeholders, with limited Return on Investment (ROI).

    - **Medium-value** impacts most of the team, occurs weekly, with a moderate ROI.

    - **High-value** impacts universally, occurs frequently, and delivers a clearly articulated high ROI, tied to key business initiatives.

2. **Assess & Place Ideas**—Together over a few sessions, discuss, assess, and place each idea under one of the value columns. As alignment is determined, assign an owner to carry any priority actions to the next stage as the process unfolds.

3. **Initial Priority Sort**—Using this framework, arrange the cards in each column by team priority. As you do so, note on each card what departments, teams, or leadership would need to weigh in on the execution of this idea.

4. **Research Level of Lift**—The assigned owner of the cards takes steps to determine the specifics it would take for this idea to become reality and the specific level of lift involved by a subject matter expert in cross-functional collaborations. For ideas that are wholly handled inside your team, determine the point person and get this data from them. This data is added to the card. It may take some time to gather this and report back.

5. **Informed Priority Sort**—Armed with the level of lift, review the priorities and set a roadmap that aligns the ideas that are top priority in each area in the sequence your team has set.

6. **What Fits the Now**—Determine the bandwidth your team and other departments have for added initiatives and choose the order of the first actions accordingly. If it is clear that two small and one medium projects are going to get a green light, use the framework to determine what is the first action and begin there.

7. **Include Later Action Spots**—There may be great ideas that don't currently make the board that join a No-Go category; anything that needs further scoping is placed on hold is Parking Lot. New ideas get their own place until the next round of assessments.

"Innovation takes a kind of unreasonableness that runs against the tendency to accommodate oneself to the reality one faces."
—George Bernard Shaw, Nobel Prize–winning playwright

Knowing Where Your Sun Shines

To bring about true results, I have identified two critical archetypes and outlined ways to optimize each for their overall success within the business. In determining the level of lift, you have an extra checkpoint to track the context of the organization. This one thing can make your garden grow and maximize your efforts, or cast a shadow that impacts the feasibility of what you are building. Leaders exist inside this extra level of awareness and it is why we focus on it here, in the Innovation and Implementation section.

When you put this framework into practice, you allow the seeds of ideas to germinate and take up space in the soil you have prepared. This minimizes the dreaded exit interview feedback–"I didn't feel like my ideas were heard." It throws off the roadblock mentality for your direct reports.

Providing sunlight to your team's ideas is your role. Your dual responsibility is also to work with your leadership to line up the necessary approvals, or sunlight, sanctioning the work your team is doing. Without this shining your way, there is work to be done upstream.

Know yourself. Know the organization. Know your team.

The payoff is rich and worth the effort. Imagine watching as your team kicks off a project that can pivot the entire organization. Perhaps they identify a workflow currently requiring thirty people x4 hrs/week that can be replaced with an AI solution! What ideas are out there that could make that kind of difference? What can be done with that newfound time?

For all of this to work, the leader must have a vision. The innovations and implementation must align with that vision. When that alignment happens, and the team is set up for success with the right innovators and implementers, and you manage change effectively, hire well, and provide the right training, resources, and knowledge, magic happens. Wins occur that were once unimaginable.

When you experience this, you might get hooked on innovation and implementation, just like I did.

11.1 TAKE ACTION: Build a map of your team as it is now, ask yourself: *Where are the innovating and implementing gaps?* Do you need to develop, train for adaptation, or seek new additions? Set up your Kanban Board and begin eliciting ideas for the team to engage, and add their ideas. Schedule follow-up sessions for continuing to build out and action the top priorities.

Building a world-class, high-performing team requires two key elements. There is no way around it—innovation and implementation.

Empowerment Inquiry

The inquiries below are presented to prepare you for the self-assessment that follows. Think about where you are at in terms of each, take notes, and use this information to support the self-assessment.

- Consider the recent implementations. How did they go?
- How often do you hear "I didn't know...," or "I don't have...," or "I can't determine...?"
- Has your team surprised you with what they have missed?
- How long does it take someone to ramp up to proficiency?
- Is your team executing and adapting at acceptable rates?
- Can you share on one page the output and result of your team?
- How often have you had a meaningful conversation with a team member?
- When was the last time a team member brought an idea to the table? What happened?

Empowerment: Self-Assessment

Scoring Scale:

1. **Highly Capable** (consistently excels in this area)
2. **Strong** (performs well, room for improvement)
3. **Developing** (some competence, needs growth)
4. **Needs Improvement** (struggles in this area, seeking support)
5. **Significant Opportunity for Growth** (gap identified, development plan needed)

Instructions:

- For each statement, assign a score from 1 to 5
- Total your scores for each section
- Reflect on your overall performance and identify areas for improvement

1. **Resistance to Change: When implementing changes, my team exhibits minimal resistance.**

   Score: ____

2. **Access to Knowledge: My team consistently has the necessary information and resources to perform their tasks effectively.**

   Score: ____

3. **Decision-Making Authority: Team members are empowered to make decisions appropriate to their roles without unnecessary escalation.**

   Score: ____

4. **Appropriate Tool Utilization: The team selects and uses tools and methods that are well-suited to the tasks at hand.**

   Score: ____

5. **Training and Development: Team members receive adequate training and development opportunities to excel in their roles.**

   Score: ____

6. **Performance Consistency: The team maintains a consistent level of performance, with minimal outliers.**

   Score: ____

7. **Engagement and Feedback: Team responsiveness to leader check-ins resulting in changes in behavior or performance.**

   Score: ____

8. **Innovation and Implementation: Team members frequently propose and implement new ideas that lead to measurable improvements.**

   Score: ____

   Total Score: ____

Scoring Interpretation:

- **8–16**: Your team is highly empowered. Continue to nurture this environment to maintain high performance and build leaders.
- **17–24**: Your team is moderately empowered but may benefit from targeted improvements in specific areas. Consider labs and workshops.
- **25–40**: There are significant opportunities to enhance team empowerment. Consider developing a focused action plan to address the identified gaps with support.

Reflect on your scores and identify specific areas where you can take actionable steps to further strengthen your team's performance.

PHASE 3: ENDEAVOR

From Ownership To Realization

CHAPTER 12

BUY-IN

If your team isn't bought in, you are the roadblock.

You've rallied your people around clear goals, guided them through change, and watched engagement light up your culture—but there's one final threshold to cross before momentum sticks. Imagine the moment when a team member doesn't just do the work you've asked—they own it, refine it, and drive it forward even when you're not in the room. **That shift from participation to true ownership is the heartbeat of lasting success.**

Recall a time your team checked every box yet left you wanting more, when deadlines were met but the spark was missing. You handed out playbooks and laid tracks, but the train stalled. What was missing? It wasn't skill or resources; it was that deep commitment transforming good teams into an unstoppable force.

Next, we'll explore how to unlock this level, moving beyond engagement into the realm of genuine buy-in. You'll co-create goals that ignite passion, step back without stepping away, and build a cycle of trust and ownership, catapulting your team to new heights. Let's turn alignment into advocacy and tasks into missions worth championing.

Recognizing Buy-in is as important as knowing how to intentionally generate it. You may see these blooms but not realize that you can capitalize on them as a multiplier. Look around for these indicators of natural buy-in so you can find ways to add more to your garden purposefully.

- Team members self-directing
- Clear path to meeting strategic initiatives, goals, and targets
- Drive collaboration to solve challenges
- Internalize aspirational goals
- Collaboratively developed step goals
- Fosters robust change, rampant acceptance, and unabashed execution
- Scorecards are awash in green
- Requires a leader to decentralize power
- Macro-management is the rule, and micro-management is the exception
- Observable creativity and problem-solving
- A team moving in lock-step

Are you unintentionally capping your team's potential?

When goals are set to stay within comfort zones, they limit growth instead of inspiring it. Instead of staying safe or realistic, challenge your team to redefine what's possible. Invite bold thinking, co-create stretch targets, and model belief in potential. This shift—from control to collaboration—builds ownership, sparks innovation, and leads to outcomes no one thought possible.

What's fantastic about The E3 Effect is that it's cyclical. Repeating Enable, Empower, then culminating with Endeavor generates a path that will upend your operational assumptions and make aspirational objectives materialize. When you get to Endeavor and experience buy-in, it allows a team to leap from the Norming stage to Performing, without Storming.

Think back: Have you ever had an experience where you guided a team through the journey of becoming familiar with the organization and one another, learning the resources and tools, becoming experts in them, and then performing to the point of consistently meeting and exceeding expectations? That's buy-in.

Engagement vs. Buy-In

You might be asking: *How does engagement compare to buy-in?*

First, distinct stages unfold over time. Before buy-in is possible, there must be engagement. People need access to information, context, and purpose. The simple truth: **buy-in can't happen when the "why" is missing**.

Engagement is about connection. It means someone is involved—they've opened the file, joined the meeting, and read the strategy deck. That's the starting point. But participation alone doesn't guarantee alignment. It doesn't mean they're invested.

Buy-in is deeper. It's when a team member doesn't just hear your message—they carry it forward in your absence. It's when someone acts in full alignment with the mission, even when no one is watching. Engagement gives you activity. Buy-in gives you accountability.

Here's a way to think about it:

Engagement is receiving the playbook.

Buy-in is making the play your own and delivering like the game depends on it.

If you want to build a team that executes at a high level, don't just ask, "Are they engaged?" Ask, **"Have they truly bought in?"**

However, when engagement exists without real buy-in—when someone follows the plan but doesn't believe in it—it creates friction beneath the surface. In business, it shows up as passive compliance, quiet resistance, or inconsistent execution. One detail may seem minor on its own, but repeated misalignment adds up. Over time, it weakens culture, derails strategy, and undercuts results. When action happens without agreement, cracks form. Trust fades. Momentum dies. Disengagement creeps in. Targets get missed. Teams go through the motions. Engagement without buy-in? It looks fine—until it doesn't.

One way to frame it is this: Engagement starts the conversation. Buy-in ensures it's carried forward. To fulfill the vision, your team must do more than echo the message—they have to bring it to life. We'll explore how in the next chapter.

Cultivating Buy-in Case Study

One directive included increasing credit card collection conversion from a low twenty percent. The team gathered contributing factors and analyzed data, resulting in a set of actions. The usual quality auditing, tracking, reporting, creating new scripts, and revising policies were employed. Our step goal game was strong by this point, so we had buy-in.

As step goals were missed, instead of *"why not?"* we asked: *"What are the reasons that brought us to this point?"* This identified compliance scripting that removed the card requirement to proceed. The organization declined to adjust it. Leveraging buy-in, the team took on a *focus on what we can control* mindset, which led us to a solution elsewhere in the workflow. We burst through the expected aspirational goal in a short time.

As for the things outside of the team's control: That's a leader's job. It's on you to see what can be done, and then report back to the team. By doing that, unifying the team, sharing ownership and accountability for our credit card conversion metric, trust was built. They know you're in it with them—helping them succeed, supporting them directly and indirectly, celebrating their wins, and digging into the root causes on their behalf.

Maintaining Buy-in While Implementing AI

The latest reckoning is already here; many organizations today are scrambling to, or are confronted by, implementing artificial intelligence for tasks. This is an area where the PangeaEffect has particular expertise and provides direct support to our clients. A critical part of that conversation is illustrating ways that AI will support the work, not replace the need for people entirely. The truth is that AI initiatives will shift mundane positions to engaging **new roles** beyond what the digital agent can handle.

It will redefine the workforce. The optimal path will become **artificial intelligence plus people,** not artificial-only or people-only. All of these elements will coexist in the same space. Compare this to the advent of transportation over time: from pedestrians, to horses, then bicycles, trains, and then automobiles. Now, all of these modes of conveyance coexist. Each innovation shared the intent to move people or goods from one place to another, accelerating the pace at which that work could be done. In doing so, new jobs were created. The same will happen with AI.

So, how do we strike a proper balance? We still need individuals with strong critical thinking skills to supervise, monitor, and guide the development of artificial intelligence. I believe future contexts will be shaped by three main trends:

1. We'll enter an era of **hyper-personalization** with AI, tailoring interactions based on individual wants and anticipating their needs.

2. We'll see increased **human and AI collaboration**, with AI acting as a guide, working hand-in-hand to enable both internal and external customers to achieve their goals with lower effort and faster results.

3. The majority of **company interactions will become AI-handled**. Emotional and ethical AI will play a key role in that future. We're already seeing early components of it. There are robots today that can display facial expressions; just search YouTube and you'll find examples. As for ethical AI, it will take time for laws and cultural norms to catch up, but it will become a major area of focus.

12.1 TAKE ACTION: How do you see AI impacting your business as you shape the future? What will your business look like in twelve, twenty-four, and thirty-six months? Generate and capture a few ideas.

Ask yourself: *What is my workforce's biggest fear, issue, or perceived roadblock? Am I creating space for the workforce to express themselves? As a leader, do I have someone to support me through the coming change?*

In the garden example, when the season is changing and sunlight is shifting direction, what adjustments would you make to keep your garden nurtured and blooming? Prepare for the upcoming season, plant the seeds, and water to create new blossoms. When you remove the roadblocks, the journey you are on, which follows the course of this book, will enable, empower, and generate team buy-in to fulfill a vision, which we'll discuss in the next chapter.

CHAPTER 13

FULFILLING THE VISION

If you can't see the path, neither can they.

You've built the foundation—setting expectations, guiding through change, equipping your people, and igniting innovation—and you've watched engagement and buy-in ripple through every corner of your team. Yet even the strongest framework can falter if the destination remains a mystery. A vision without a clear path is like a compass without a North.

Think back to the last time you felt electrified by a goal so vivid you could taste it—the product launch that promised to reshape the market, the strategic shift destined to redefine your team's impact, or the company mission you rallied behind. That spark of possibility is your vision, but it only matters if everyone can see exactly where you're pointing.

Vision Realization and Continuous Improvement

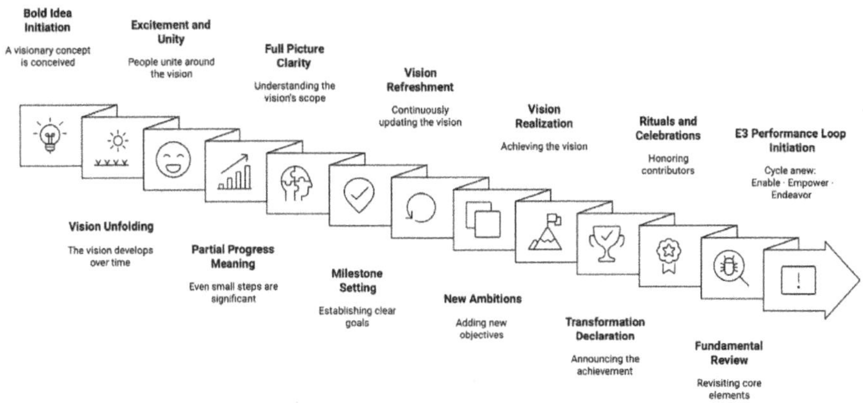

In this chapter, we'll explore how to translate big-picture aspirations into a roadmap so tangible that each person knows, not just what to do, but why it matters. You'll learn to internalize strategic initiatives, synthesize them into a guiding philosophy, and plant the seeds of clarity that let your team navigate the path with confidence. Let's turn lofty ideals into daily action—and fulfill the strategic vision together.

Most leaders at the highest levels within the organization understand the **goals**, **mission**, and **values** of strategic initiatives. Beyond understanding lies endeavoring to internalize and synthesize it into an overarching philosophy: This is who we are, this is how we work, and these are the outcomes we will deliver. This aids in assessing the most significant problems that the organization is facing.

It may feel, if your organization is big, that you have seen these goals, but struggle to connect directly. Create your own aspirational goal, and then the step goals to arrive there. Where can you start? From your perspective, what is the organization's biggest issue?

Just as you have provided discernment training opportunities for your direct reports, place yourself in a session with your leader, focusing on, first and foremost, **alignment** in this area. Build an idea that addresses this top issue that is crystal clear on the strategic initiative and how it aligns with the mission, goals, vision, and values. Then, you want to socialize that up the chain of command to ensure there's buy-in. Any lack of buy-in from your leader equates to little sunlight. Adjust until you have the full force shining on you and your efforts. Now you are afforded the opportunity to have traction and grow as intended.

Check in with your leader—or anywhere else within the chain—to stay aligned cross-functionally. As you socialize, you plant seeds for where you're going. Till the garden until the soil is prepared and rich with nutrients. Plant the right seeds, providing aligned expectations. To yield an oak tree, you must have the space. Buy-in provides ample space for your efforts to grow.

Managing Disruptors

What is the antithesis of engagement? Disruptors. Earlier, we talked about change management. Identifying individuals as **detractors**, **neutral**, **influencers**, or **advocates** allows for optimal handling of each and for the blooms of culture to stay healthy. The same approach applies to buy-in. A gap in engagement or buy-in shows up as **disruptors**.

One recent podcast featured behavioral scientists [can't remember the exact ones]who studied the number of people in an organization it takes to shift the culture from positive to negative, from functional to dysfunctional, or from Norming or Performing to Storming. They found that one disruptor within a team of five can have a significant impact. If you have two disruptors who are not bought in, you're going to notice it. If you have three, you're probably not going to maintain forward momentum without significant effort and without disengaging those who lack buy-in. Remember that number: three.

It applies to groups of one hundred. Any solo disruptor will remain discounted, but a trio? People will take notice. Influencing will occur. This anecdote underscores the importance of keeping the weeds of distractors cleared out when they are not established enough to take root.

Notice when you have someone who's not bought in. Watch for disengagement, **disenfranchisement**, dissatisfaction, or viewing things from a completely different perspective. Even if well-intentioned, they deserve attention and support. Left to spin, those individuals are ripe to become disruptors if not addressed.

Are you mindful of who's in your group and your team? Realize the rest are monitoring how you mitigate these forces. Do you address it directly? Do you let them get away with it for a while? Do you ignore it and just hope it'll go away? Do you take decisive action? Don't wait until there are 3, it's too late then. The team will value action over inaction.

To fulfill a vision, you must have buy-in. Remember: Where there's smoke, there's fire, so you must address it to protect your valuable buy-in.

A Vision for All

A worthy vision starts as a bold idea—one so ambitious it requires everyone's effort. It unfolds over time and ignites genuine excitement, uniting people around a shared goal. Even partial progress becomes profoundly meaningful.

Begin by stepping back to see the full picture: outline how each element connects to your aspiration. With that clarity, set concrete milestones that guide every team member forward.

What sets world-class organizations apart is their willingness to refresh and extend their vision continuously. By layering new ambitions onto current objectives, they keep the ultimate goal just beyond reach—not for lack of success, but to inspire courage and drive toward ever-greater horizons.

Examples: Meta, or Facebook, has significantly evolved its vision over time. Its initial big idea that became their vision was "connecting the world." This evolved to the "Metaverse Vision," the next evolution of the Internet. They changed their name to create buy-in, focus, and passion around this vision. Meta's vision is currently to build "personal superintelligence for everyone." Microsoft's initial vision in 1975 was "A computer on every desk." By the 1990s, this vision had largely been realized, and they created a new one, building on what they had delivered: "To help people and businesses around the world realize their full potential." As that vision was fulfilled, it shifted again to "an intelligent cloud and an intelligent edge infused with AI."

What happens after the vision is realized and the monumental difference is made? Think about it, the enterprise is operating at a new level. Leadership may have turned over or become reliant on this quantum leap for baseline success. What then? Have you started to phase in the new vision, building on the earlier objectives? **A roadmap to keep the flywheel of success turning will keep your team performing at its highest level** and the pivot will be easier.

Once your vision is realized, literally made real, you've elevated the organization to a new level. Yet, that higher standard can quickly feel like the norm. To avoid coasting or stalling, weave in fresh objectives and map out a clear path so momentum never stalls. Start by formally declaring the transformation complete: honor every contributor and give stakeholders their victory lap. Skipping these rituals risks turning extraordinary results into mere expectations. Then circle back to your fundamentals—revisit culture, ready the soil, and choose the seeds for what comes next. Only after that should you replay the E3 Performance loop: enable the right conditions, empower your people with genuine ownership, and endeavor together toward your next summit. This simple cycle keeps everyone aligned, motivated, and primed for the journey ahead.

13.1 TAKE ACTION: Start drafting bold goals that truly excite you and your team. Share those ideas, gather honest feedback, and refine until they spark real enthusiasm. Sketch your "garden," listing current assets alongside future needs, and display it where everyone can see it. Finally, invite an outsider to ask tough questions—those unbiased perspectives will sharpen your focus and keep your next vision rooted in reality.

The term **Endeavor** focuses on getting results, hinging on two specific topics we introduced in this chapter–the fundamental aspects of **buy-in** and **fulfilling the vision**. With these in place, it is time to turn to results.

At one organization, we hosted a department-level monthly business review, inviting leaders from every other department, along with a select group of key stakeholders who regularly interacted with our team. We had different attendees each month, and what I found was that when we sent out a reminder ahead of time—along with some high-level bullet points outlining the agenda—we had higher attendance than when we simply held the meeting and presented without notice.

Making Progress Visible

At the end of every meeting, we sent out the presentation and provided an opportunity for anyone to reach out to us one-on-one or as a group for follow-up. Later, when questions arose (especially during performance reviews, which are often very important), we already had a concrete and tangible set of deliverables to share. We could simply hand them over and say, "Here's what I accomplished this year. Here's what I achieved this quarter, this month. Here's what we completed, and here's what we're working on now."

When you have that kind of documentation, you're fulfilling your vision of creating both the work experience and life results that matter to you. Remember: everyone listens to their own channel—WIIFM, or "What's In It For Me?" What do *you* hear when you tune into that channel for yourself? Let's set you up for success, then you'll see results shine and thrive from there.

I wish you the best on your journey. May your successes exceed your imagination, and may what follows with you and behind you generate incredible results and success for everyone involved.

Phase 3 Self-Assessment

Rating:

1. **Highly Capable** (I consistently excel in this area, a main source of acknowledgement from leaders)

2. **Strong** (I perform well, but know I have key gaps to address)

3. **Developing** (I have some experience; an area where I get feedback calling for growth)

4. **Needs Improvement** (I struggle in this area; notice it may be holding me back)

5. **Significant Opportunity for Growth** (I have identified this as outside my natural skill set; valuable to develop this area)

Instructions:

- Rank each group 1-5
- Use Scale to Determine
- Identify Your Two Weakest Elements in Each Area

Buy-in:

1. **How readily do team members accept and display agreement with step goals and milestones?**

   Score: ____

2. **Do you primarily have advocates, neutral participants, or resistance when driving change?**

   Score: ____

3. **How independently can your team or colleagues contribute to shaping goals and initiatives?**

   Score: ____

4. **Are you enabling collaborative problem-solving or unintentionally placing limits on innovation?**

   Score: ____

5. **Is success acknowledged and celebrated, reinforcing engagement?**

   Score: ____

Fulfilling the Vision

6. **Is the vision clearly defined, with a structured roadmap that team members understand?**

   Score: ____

7. **Do you effectively communicate, refine, and adjust the vision as needed?**

   Score: ____

8. **Have you proactively gained buy-in from key stakeholders, including peers, leaders, or executives?**

   Score: ____

9. **Are potential disruptors identified and addressed before they derail progress?**

   Score: ____

10. **Are team members aware of how their work connects to the broader strategic goals?**

    Score: ____

Getting Results

11. **Are target metrics and objectives being met on a consistent basis?**

    Score: ____

12. **Are all team members actively contributing to success, or are performance gaps affecting progress?**

    Score: ____

13. **Is there a structured system for tracking, reporting, and optimizing results?**

    Score: ____

14. **Are barriers to success identified early and addressed effectively?**

    Score: ____

15. **Are you continuously refining processes to elevate performance and set new benchmarks?**

    Score: ____

    Total Score: ____

Interpreting Your Score (Sum of All Ratings, 15–75 Scale)

- **15–30: Well-Established Leadership Practices** – You are driving strong alignment, engagement, and results. Continue building on this foundation.
- **31–45:** You are on the right track, with some areas that could benefit from additional attention.
- **46–60:** Strengthening your approach in key areas will help improve team effectiveness and results.
- **61–75:** Focused effort in these areas will create meaningful improvements in leadership impact and team performance.

This assessment serves as a practical reflection tool for leaders at all levels to evaluate and enhance their team alignment, vision execution, and results-driven performance.

Awareness is only the beginning. The real impact comes when you **put it into practice**. To build on the work you've already done, **visit**

PangeaEffect.com and complete **My Roadmap**. This brief, guided primer translates your assessment into your **first actionable steps** for building buy-in, fulfilling the vision, and getting results. For you, it may be the preview that sparks momentum — or the **breakthrough insight** you've been waiting for. Either way, it's where **transformation** in your organization stops being theoretical and starts **becoming real**.

CONCLUSION

Yours to Build. Bound for Breakthrough.

You've gone from preparing the ground you stand on, your culture, to sowing the seeds of achievement with specific milestones, careful interviews, and solid expectations. You came to view change not simply as a mechanical process, but as a deeply human journey, guiding your team through the five stages of change: denial, anger, bargaining, depression, and acceptance, stages that together bring about transformation.

You created a unified source of truth that allows knowledge to circulate effortlessly, managed empowerment in relation to risk, and honed critical judgment to ensure everyone stays securely on course.

You subsequently made learning a way of life, converting training from inactive slides into practical application, and observed as skills flourished in your team, moving from deliberate effort to instinctive expertise.

You developed the ability to identify gaps—be they systemic or personal—and address them with precision and understanding. Involvement sparked the fire; satisfaction turned it into a constant blaze.

You noticed that innovation and execution enhance each other when developers, advocates, and analysts coalesce with the integral innovators and implementers.

You marked buy-in as the point when your team ceased following directions and started to take responsibility for the mission independently.

Ultimately, you charted each ambition on a tangible route, ensuring that no one confused dreams with actual outcomes.

Each chapter has centered on a single goal: transforming intention into effect. Your voice as a leader establishes the atmosphere—each word you say and action you demonstrate influences who your people evolve into. True magic occurs when you merge clear direction with empathy, firmness with adaptability, and meticulousness with interpersonal bonds.

As you finish this book and return to your organization, keep in mind **the culture as a garden analogy: fertile soil, aligned and abundant sunlight, thoughtfully selected seeds, and consistent care to produce the best yield.** Your development represents that nourished earth. Organizational alignment is the sunlight. The processes and frameworks are the tools you use to tend to the growth. And your ongoing care—through coaching, celebration, course correction, and quiet encouragement—brings the gardener's devotion– turning sprouts into a thriving crop of world-class, high-performing teams that sustain their excellence over time.

Every business, team, and individual is on their own unique journey. This book is about making that journey meaningful. It's about setting a course that makes a difference. It's about creating a story you'll look back on later in life with great satisfaction.

This is how you powerfully share what you've accomplished, what you will achieve, and what the future holds—even the parts you can't yet imagine. Did you identify ways to be *unreasonable* with yourself and generate aspirations and goals bigger than you can currently imagine? Great!

Instead of asking, *How am I going to do that?* This process is about becoming the leader who will generate that aspiration in others then charting that answer together..

It's about taking the steps and using the methods that will move you forward, milestone by milestone, toward that big, bold vision. This book shows you *how*. But without knowing *who* you will be, the doing and the having might not amount to much.

So, here's my encouragement: Go back. Revisit the chapters that align with your opportunity areas. Review the activities and the results you created. Each element in Take Action 13.2 is mapped to actionable insights from this book.

When you focus on the topics, activities and insights by priority according to your weakest areas, you begin to shape your *being* as you leverage being curious, reflective, and willing to step outside your comfort zone. All the real prizes in life come from saying *yes*, even when *no* feels like the safer answer. So say yes. Get into action.

I promise you: if you stay committed, you will generate incredible results. When you're challenged or confronted, seek out support. Come back to these pages. Reach out to PangeaEffect. Seek the resources you need to have your breakthrough, so you can continue the journey toward the outcome *you* said you wanted.

This is not a wish. This is not just hope. This is *doable.*

How? Do the work, and the results will follow. Have an amazing journey, and know that you are supported every step of the way—through this book, through your community, if not your community, then through *mine*.

We are here to empower your success, to help you build a life you love while you lead a team that loves what they do. Let's go win.

To everyone who made it to the conclusion: first, I want to honor you. Completing something you've started is powerful. It proves you are committed to building high-performing teams. It demonstrates that you are someone others can learn from.

When you show up for yourself, you do the same for others—it's clear you're here to make a difference, not just for yourself but also for your organization and the communities you care about most. I respect that. I appreciate that. And I acknowledge *you* for being someone who stepped up and took this challenge on.

My hope for you is that you find your momentum by taking these first steps, and reaching farther than you ever thought you could—because your vision is bigger than you may have ever imagined.

And with that, the world is yours. You *can* create, *can* be, *can* do, and *can* have all that you desire. What you have already accomplished is amazing. Your leadership makes a difference.

You are not on your own. At any moment, support is available to help you step up to the next level. To have breakthroughs in your unbreakable moments. To create visions worthy of your time, effort, desires, and dreams.

PangaeaEffect is an organization built to simplify transformation, generate big breakthroughs, and build high-performing teams. Through a simple conversation, a series of connections to support your endeavors, or a long-term project, we're here to partner and make your efforts bold enough and big enough to be worth your investment. We're here to advise, guide, or walk with you over the long term.

We are your strength when you feel like you have none. To get in touch with us, scan the QR code at the end of this book.

Reaching out is both an honor and an opportunity: an honor to hear from you, and an opportunity to support you in having a breakthrough in generating your greatest vision and the results that follow. If you're not in a place where you're ready to create your biggest vision, I encourage you—with everything I've provided here— start with a small, *winnable* vision.

- "I'm going to make one material change this week."

- "By the end of next week, I'll complete one key task."
- "By the end of this month, my team will brainstorm ideas for a future breakthrough."

Now it's your turn to keep growing. Start small. Pick an activity from your roadmap and apply it today. Nourish it, watch it take root, move to the next. Over time, you'll look back to see a landscape transformed: thriving, resilient, a team capable of reaching heights you once only imagined. That is the promise of leadership done expertly, and the journey you're on has just begun.

Wherever you are on your path, use *this* moment to generate your greatest vision: Be the standard. Do with discipline. Generate the team that others follow.

Lead with clarity. Build with purpose. Deliver what endures.
With The E³ Effect.

THANK YOU FOR PURCHASING AND READING

THE E3 EFFECT

Scan the QR Code to access your exclusive reader benefits:

- Join live **webinars and peer discussions** with like-minded leaders
- Explore **tools and frameworks** used to build high-performing teams
- Receive a **discount** for the **E3 Performance Summit: Where Leaders Become Multipliers**
- Be the first to hear about the **audiobook release**
- Claim **bulk order perks** for your team
- Schedule a **Fireside Chat, Panel, or Speaking Engagement**
- Share the **E3 Leader Assessment** with your team
- Learn about **E3 Effect Trainer Certification** and **exclusive training programs**

Visit our resources page for additional leadership tools, articles, and insights designed to elevate your leadership and team performance.

TheE3Effect.com

Ready to build a world-class team?

PangeaEffect delivers a performance multiplier effect — blending people, process, and technology to transform operations, build world-class call centers, and empower leaders to scale with clarity and confidence.

PANGEAEFFECT - Advancing Technology and Accelerating Performance

www.ingramcontent.com/pod-product-compliance
Lightning Source LLC
Chambersburg PA
CBHW021929190326
41519CB00009B/955

9781968250393